A Heretic's guide to Eternity

A Heretic's Guide to Eternity

Spencer Burke
and Barry Taylor

Foreword by
Brian McLaren

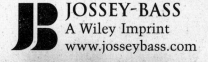

JOSSEY-BASS
A Wiley Imprint
www.josseybass.com

Published by Jossey-Bass
A Wiley Imprint
989 Market Street, San Francisco, CA 94103-1741   www.josseybass.com

Jossey-Bass books and products are available through most bookstores. To contact Jossey-Bass directly call our Customer Care Department within the U.S. at 800-956-7739, outside the U.S. at 317-572-3986, or fax 317-572-4002.

Jossey-Bass also publishes its books in a variety of electronic formats. Some content that appears in print may not be available in electronic books.

All scripture quotations, unless otherwise indicated, are taken from the HOLY BIBLE, NEW INTERNATIONAL VERSION®. NIV®. Copyright © 1973, 1978, 1984 by International Bible Society. Used by permission of Zondervan. All rights reserved.

Scripture quotations marked "NKJV™" are taken from the New King James Version®. Copyright © 1982 by Thomas Nelson, Inc. Used by permission. All rights reserved.

Scripture quotations marked NASB are taken from the New American Standard Bible®. Copyright © 1960, 1962, 1963, 1968, 1971, 1972, 1973, 1975, 1977, 1995 by The Lockman Foundation. Used by permission. (www.Lockman.org)

Library of Congress Cataloging-in-Publication Data
Burke, Spencer.
A heretic's guide to eternity / Spencer Burke and Barry Taylor;
foreword by Brian McLaren.
p. cm.
Includes bibliographical references and index.
ISBN-13: 978-0-7879-8359-8 (cloth)
ISBN-10: 0-7879-8359-4 (cloth)
1. Salvation—Christianity. 2. Future life—Christianity. 3. Eternity. 4. Postmodernism—Religious aspects—Christianity. I. Taylor, Barry, date. II. Title.
BT751.3.B87 2006
230—dc22   2006014171

Printed in the United States of America
FIRST EDITION
HB Printing 10 9 8 7 6 5 4 3 2 1

contents

SECTION ONE

questioning grace:
The future of faith

SECTION TWO

Questioning What We Know:
New Horizons of Faith

SECTION THREE

Living in Grace:
Mystical Responsibility

foreword

S omeone recently sent me one of those clever top-ten lists that you always see floating around the Internet. It was entitled, "Top Ten Reasons Beer Is Better Than Religion." My favorite five out of the top ten are

1. No one will kill you for not drinking Beer.
2. Beer has never caused a major war.
3. Nobody's ever been burned at the stake, hanged, or tortured over his brand of Beer.
4. You don't have to wait 2000+ years for a second Beer.
5. There are laws saying Beer labels can't lie to you.

Now I'm not advertising beer, but I am advocating that we who have a sincere faith in God realize that there are a number of downsides to religion . . . some of which are implied by the humorous beer list. There's a grim historical track record of religious inebriation that, like drunk driving, has taken or ruined too many lives already.

Even those of us who are deeply and passionately devoted to the life, work, teachings, and example of Jesus Christ must admit that way too much bad stuff has already been done in his name. I thought of this recently when a Jewish friend said, "You know, I really think Jesus was from God. I think he was a true prophet. I think we Jews were wrong to reject him." But then he added, "But after 2,000 years of Christian anti-Semitism, you can't expect us to sign up right away for the virgin birth or the doctrine of the trinity." Even those of us who are firm believers in the virgin birth and the doctrine of the trinity have to hear what he is saying.

Of course, the word "heretic" is a serious word. It has been used in various inquisitions to legitimize the kinds of horrific things beer drinkers would never do for love of beer. Spencer Burke and Barry Taylor, in choosing it for the title of this book, are indulging in dangerous, risky language. Why would anybody take that kind of outrageous risk?

I guess for the same reason that the prophets in the Hebrew Scriptures did outrageous things—from cooking on excrement to walking around naked to marrying a prostitute to confronting a king for his cover-up of immoral activity. (I won't even mention how Jesus committed scandalous outrage after scandalous outrage—intentionally healing on the Sabbath, excusing the breaking of religious rituals and taboos, talking to the wrong people—even touching them!—speaking of the Temple being less than essential for the future, and so on.)

Why would anyone risk a dangerous title like this for a needed book like this? I guess for the same reason my friend Tony Campolo (in a story that has many apocryphal versions) earned a reputation for speaking to groups of prim and proper Christian leaders and saying something like this: "Millions of children are dying in poverty, and you don't give a #$@%!" As faces blanched, he would add wryly, "And to prove my point, you're more upset that I said #$@% than you are that millions of children are dying in poverty."

Why use such risky language in the title? I guess for the same reason that the great author Flannery O'Connor wrote stories with really weird, creepy, disturbed, and dysfunctional characters. When readers are nearly blind, she explained, you have to draw exaggerated lines. Otherwise they can't see anything at all. Søren Kierkegaard said something similar when he talked about the need for indirect theological "butt-kicking." (His exact language was more Campolo-esque.) People who are held firmly in the grip of an illusion, he said, need an indirect but real jolt to be awakened.

I imagine that the blogs and maybe even religious broadcasting airwaves will soon be buzzing with scandalous outrage that Spencer and Barry have used the word "heretic" in their title. Maybe the risk they're taking won't be worth it, as scores of serious, concerned people try to take the logs out of the authors' eyes, unaware that they might even have a tiny metal shaving in their own. But maybe their risk will pay off—especially if some people do more than react to the scandalous title and actually read this book and realize, not what's wrong with heresy (which is obvious to almost everybody), but what's so often wrong with religion, including "our" religion (whichever that might be).

The serious and concerned religious folks who would be most prone to attack Spencer and Barry for their title should, perhaps, realize that they are doing them a great favor, an act of courage and charity. They are showing those religious folks what about them is turning off and driving away millions of people . . . often including their own children and grandchildren. Those being turned off won't tell them these things because . . . because they've tried it in the past and the results weren't good. Instead, they just keep their distance and try to be polite, even though they're usually somewhere between disappointed and disgusted and terrified.

It's easy for inquisition-launchers to go on fault-finding missions; they have lots of practice and they're really good at it. What's more challenging, and, regarding this book, much more worthwhile, is to instead go on a truth-finding mission. And yes, even in a book with "heretic" in the title, I believe any honest reader can find much truth worth seeking.

Perhaps even those who have become legally inebriated on the hops and malt of fault-finding, those who are inquisition-aholics but think they can quit anytime . . . perhaps even they might get a brief glimpse in the mirror in these pages, a glimpse that will do them good. And they might realize that, contrary to the title, this book isn't really about heresy or eternity: it's about . . . well, it's about something far better than either beer or religion. I'll leave you to fig-ure out what that is when you turn the page and read what's been fermenting in Spencer's and Barry's hearts.

May 2006   Brian McLaren

acknowledgments

For me, creating a book is much like the art of photography. When I first began as a photographer, I was committed to a pure execution, doing everything myself—from taking the picture to developing, printing, and framing it. As time went on, I realized the benefit of collaboration. With that experience, I approach my writing in the same way. It is a collaborative engagement, not a solo effort, and it's essential to celebrate all of the people who leave their fingerprints on this project.

I thank those who have taught me the basics, helping form my spiritual foundation—my parents, Bob and Claire Burke; my in-laws, Dave and Jan Coleman; my mentors, Jack Hafer, Ray Botello, and Kim Storm; churches, schools, seminaries, and so many individuals. Without their guidance, I would approach life in a different way.

I also thank those who have helped me think beyond the basics. The wit, insights, and courage of people I've traveled with, learned from, and worked with have been instrumental in my concepts of this new emerging spirituality. Though too numerous to mention by name here, I am indebted to all those mentioned in the pages of this book, and the list continues to grow.

This book is also a reflection of the people I've shared life with and adventured with—my wife, Lisa; our children, Alden and Grace; those who have helped me understand the community of faith, including Matt and Krista, Dave and Beth, Robert and Betsy; Todd Littleton, Brian Dowd, and all the participants in ETREK; those who express their wide varieties of opinions and ideas on TheOOZE.com; and those who have been instrumental in TheOOZE—Malcolm Hawker, Shayna Metzner, Alan Hartung, Jim and Tammy Schoch, Jordon Cooper, and Charlie Wear. Like Polaroid photos taken before you commit to the composition, the wide variety of places where I was able to test and refine my ideas have also been important—pubs, conferences, workshops, small gatherings.

My thanks also go to David Sanford, who partnered with me to move beyond the Polaroids and find a wider audience. As a literary agent, his wisdom, insight, support, and belief in me and the vision of my images have been of inestimable value.

Sheryl Fullerton at Jossey-Bass has filled the role of patron, supporting this work and providing the resources to take it beyond the Polaroids. She has been supportive, inspirational, and willing to give freedom to explore new schools of thought that challenge our perspectives, ideas, and realities.

Barry Taylor was to be the technician who turned the ideas into substance, but he evolved into so much more—a great partner in the lab with research, execution, depth, and wisdom, and the art director whose point of view resulted in a much broader, more imaginative book. I can't express enough how much I value the friendship, the late-night conversations, and the wonderful highs and lows of discovery I've shared with Barry throughout this process. Thanks also to Donna and Rylee for their generosity and patience.

Colleen Pepper was the editor who made sure the image was alive, the colors true, vibrant, and resonant with reality. Her work allowed the image to pop out, framing the raw image to achieve the greatest impact. She understood what I was thinking and translated that into a living picture.

Rebekah Clark was the retouch artist who edited the tiniest details when everyone else had fuzzy eyes, rechecking the focus and correcting flaws that detracted from the image.

My deep appreciation also goes to the rest of the team at Sanford Communications, Inc., and to all at Jossey-Bass, who have been an amazing support team throughout this project.

You'll notice the text is written from my perspective, but to assume that any one sentence or phrase is the work of a purist, in the lab alone, would be to underestimate the abilities of a collaborative team. As you read, what you see is an amalgam of all the people who have been involved in bringing this book to fruition, behind the scenes.

S. B.

TO MY wife, Lisa.

Your kindness, support, and friendship have sustained me.

Your smile, wisdom, and skill have guided me.

Your passion, commitment, and love have inspired me.

S.B.

introduction

It is the customary fate of new truths
to begin as heresies.

—Thomas Huxley

May you live in interesting times." This greeting once used by Chinese revolutionaries may sound friendly, but it wasn't. To wish that someone would live in interesting times was to hope that he or she would experience great transition or upheaval—hardly a blessing in a country that took pride in its long, uninterrupted history and stable way of life.

Today, we too live in interesting times. We may not have asked for it, but continuous change is a fact of life in our society. As those who have transitioned from the second half of the twentieth century into the new millennium, we have already lived through the demise of one great revolution of the human spirit and currently find ourselves entering another.

This first revolution was called the Enlightenment by some people and modernity by others. But whatever its name, this period birthed the scientific worldview along with the scientific method. Before long, the controlled experiment ruled the day. Eventually, there was little room left for a traditional God-centered view of nature or even belief in a deity. During this age, the secular seemed to be developed at the expense of the sacred. While religion remained on the cultural landscape, it was in a greatly weakened state—a mere vapor trail of a once vibrant culture-shaping force.

The second great shift is happening as I write this book. Although it is much less noticeable than the first, it is no less real. A reversal of sorts is occurring. God is now back in the picture, but in vastly different manifestations than before. Some people call this new period of time postmodernity; others call it hypermodernity. Again, no matter what label one applies, the fact remains that the West is reordering itself.

There seems to be a general sense in our culture that something went wrong during the last revolution. Modernity did not deliver on all of its promises. A world built on scientific achievement alone has proved not to be sufficient. Just because science can affirm what is before our eyes in nature does not necessarily mean nature is all there is.

Science has been all about vision over the years—telescopes and microscopes, facts and figures. It has charted and explored the smallest organisms to the vast reaches of the universe, but it still cannot see everything. Thoughts and feelings, for instance, remain elusive and hard to pin down. Much of the human experience cannot be explained by biology alone. Life, it seems, is more than test tubes and chemical compounds—and this is where much of the world has turned its attention over the past decade or so. People are increasingly interested in the soul, the spirit, and the nonmaterial.

That is not to say that science has not contributed greatly to the world we currently inhabit or that it doesn't continue to do

> Life is more than test tubes and chemical compounds. . . . people are increasingly interested in the soul, the spirit, and the nonmaterial.

so. I am not a Luddite antimodernist. I have no desire to return to a prescientific world of spells, cures, and leeches. It is just that it has become increasingly clear to me, as well as to many others, that there are weaknesses in trusting only what can be studied through the five senses.

The scientific view is the skeletal form of modernity, and it has influenced and shaped every aspect of our lives. Science and scientific rationalism offered us two things that were meant to replace our hunger for the divine—secularism and technology.

Secularism is a way of looking at the world apart from the language and rule of the gods. It was meant to be liberating, freeing us from superstition and opening up a universe of opportunities previously held in check by the whims of the divine. The idea that humans are in control of their own destinies was the rallying cry of the modern age. Under secularism, religion continued to exist, but it had a much less prominent role. Rather than being the central core around which we built our lives—the model for thousands of years—religion and sacred pursuits became privatized and pushed to the margins of society. Science took the place of God, offering answers and giving meaning to life.

Secularism's partner, technology, pitched the assurance of a better future and the guarantee of unending progress. In fact, the results were so bright, we had to invent sunglasses to protect us from the light of its promise! But even so, technological progress took us only so far. Although it cannot be denied that many discoveries gifted to us through technology have made life more comfortable for millions of people, science has also helped create weapons of mass destruction—weapons that threaten the very future of human existence.

Technology, it seems, hasn't been entirely effective in making the world a better place. In fact, some say the twentieth century was the most violent in human history. Two world wars, along with devastating famines, AIDS, and other calamities, would seem to provide obvious evidence that we have not yet perfected this planet.

Whatever the statistics, faith in modernity's future slumped at the end of the twentieth century.

At the same time, however, science and technology are actually a part of the reason for the renewed interest in spirituality. Science has also shifted radically over the years. We no longer live in a Newtonian world. We have a post-Einsteinian view of the universe. We live in the era of quantum physics, and it offers a much more complicated picture of life. Thanks to science, it has been said, the twentieth century began in certainty and ended in uncertainty. Never again will we be so sure of ourselves, so confident in our own understanding about things, so full of pride at our accomplishments. Science has let the mystery in.

In a seminal essay on religion and knowledge, the French philosopher Jacques Derrida advanced the theory that the very technologies we use have contributed to the revival of the divine in our times. "Because one increasingly uses artifacts and prostheses of which one is totally ignorant, the space of such technical experience tends to become more animistic, magical, mystical." Or as Erik Davis says, the "primary concern remains the spiritual imagination and how it mutates in the face of changing technologies."

There seems to be something to this idea. Technology has mysteries all its own. Of course, the more scientific among us will immediately feel compelled to offer some theory to explain how it all works, but nonetheless, when you turn on the television and pictures flood into your living room, there is a mysterious aspect to it, even when the theories have been fully explained. It is a wild theory that electric currents can transmit images and sounds that we can access through a box in our homes. Or think about one of the most popular technological devices of the twenty-first century so far, the iPod Shuffle. It is the first piece of technology to make randomness an integral part of its function. You switch the power on, press play, and you don't know which song will come next. What comes out of the accompanying earphones is simply the result of random programming.

Much has already been written about the strange phenomena that many people have experienced with their iPods. There seems to be an uncanny symbiosis between the listener's emotional state and the kind of music that plays. (Just Google the terms *iPod* and *mystery* and see what you get.) The rationalists will immediately offer explanations noting that the randomness is actually not random. The music, they will explain, was downloaded by the listening individual, and it is probably coincidence that there seems to be a link between one's emotional state and the music playing through the iPod. Nevertheless, that doesn't negate the strange feeling of hearing the perfect song for one's present emotional state at the mere push of a button.

As we expand our relationship with technology, the opportunities to access new ideas, new thoughts, and new mysteries seem to be growing exponentially. However, technology can lead us only so far in our journey. It may have opened the door to mystery, but we still have to walk through that door. And that seems to be what's happening today. More than ever, it seems, people are interested in all kinds of transcendence.

Anne Rice, famed author of vampire novels, has just released her latest novel. This time around, she's picked a new central character: Jesus. In fact, *Christ the Lord: Out of Egypt* is the first in a series of books on the life of Jesus that the author says will be the focus of the remainder of her writing life. "Something is in the air," she said in an interview on NBC's *Today* show. "People want to talk about Jesus. They want to talk about religion. And they are interested in spirituality."

If you were to watch Christian TV or listen to some of the most prominent evangelists, you would likely hear talk of the "coming revival." But could it be that the revival is already upon us? It just doesn't fit the old categories. It is not a revival of traditional Christianity, although it does reap some of the rewards. It is a revival of the spiritual on a completely new level. I will speak more of this in Chapter One.

The philosopher Archibald MacLeish declared that "a world ends when its metaphor has died," and modernity's metaphor has surely died. Belief in endless progress through science is over. Those of us who haven't fully realized it yet are simply experiencing the cultural lag that naturally occurs when we can't fully face the future.

In the Old Testament, Israel was always wanting to go back to Egypt. The people were convinced that even though captivity was bad, it was still more secure than an unknown future in a land no one had seen. We share that tendency to look back. Often we humans hold on to systems that are no longer as vital or as meaningful as they once were because we cannot envisage a way forward without them.

Take politics, for example. To say that Western culture has lost faith in government would be a huge understatement. The truth, of course, is that the public has lost faith in all kinds of institutions in our culture, including science, technology, media, and business. Still, in the realm of politics, the evidence is especially hard to ignore. In the United States, voter turnout is decreasing with every election, especially among young people. In spite of well-intentioned efforts to get younger voters to the polls, including Rock the Vote, young Americans just don't believe in government the way their parents and grandparents did. In the current age of special-interest lobbying, spin-doctoring, and market-research-driven campaigning, cynicism runs rampant.

With the possible exception of right-wing fundamentalists and others who find government affirming their interests, most people I know roll their eyes when the subject of politics is raised. It isn't that people don't care about politics; it's that they no longer believe the system is able to serve a diverse populace. Instead, they perceive of government as serving only the interests of those in the existing power structures.

I would suggest the same is true of religion. As with government, many people no longer count on religion to deliver on its promises and provide meaning and motivation. It, too, has a tendency to serve only its own. Many believe it has lost its imagination and its ability to offer any genuine hope for a better future.

But things are changing. As I mentioned earlier, God is coming back into the picture in new and different ways. While some may perceive this second great shift in our culture as a threat to Christianity, I and others like me see it as an opportunity—a pivotal moment, even, in the future of the faith.

> Many people no longer count on religion to deliver on its promises and provide meaning and motivation.

Two major pivotal moments for Christianity were the issue of slavery in the 1800s and the civil rights movement of the 1950s and 1960s. The social and religious upheaval generated by the rise of the civil rights movement brought the church to a place where it had to examine itself and decide, at last, to say no to its support of segregation. Although the issue had been around for a long time, cultural events forced the church's hand. It became impossible for the church to reconcile its position supporting racism and injustice with the gospel it claimed to represent. Cultural forces compelled the church into new theological reflection, which in turn produced new theological positions. The people marching in the streets forced the church to demonstrate in word—and deed—its position on issues it had previously avoided or ignored.

The future of religion is up for debate. We would argue that the rise of fundamentalism in all faiths is only helping to underscore how threatened the idea of religion is. Fundamentalism thrives on declaring what is not of God and particularly *who* is not of God. This is an issue of concern not just for religious communities but also for our entire global community. Thankfully, people are increasingly saying no to these kinds of relationships to God while continuing to consider the idea of the divine. They're looking for hope, looking for answers, and seeking to build new types of relationships with each other and the divine.

At this point in our history, I believe God is to be questioned as much as obeyed, created again and not simply worshiped. Our views must be continually revised, reconsidered, and debated. Spirituality in the twenty-first century is not etched in stone but fashioned out of the fabrics of our lives in new and ever-changing permutations. This is the focus and the hope of this book.

> spirituality in the twenty-first century is not etched in stone but fashioned out of the fabrics of our lives in new and ever-changing permutations.

There is a funny and poignant ad playing on television at present. It is an ad for an investment and brokerage company called the Scottish Bank. It features a group of businessmen at lunch discussing the intricacies of the Heimlich maneuver. As they argue over the various dos and don'ts of the lifesaving theory, one of the diners begins to choke on some food. While the rest of the diners argue over what should or should not be done, the man continues to choke until at last someone from another table comes over, performs the maneuver, and saves the man's life.

I see this as a metaphor for the way in which people are approaching issues of faith today. The shift is from talking to doing. I believe people are tired of all the talk and the constant bickering over details. In fact, they're so tired of it that they're increasingly willing to rethink some of the old dividing lines. This brings us to the subject of heresy.

Why pick the word *heretic* as a device for a book on the future of religion? The word itself conjures up images of much darker times. What was the fate of those who willfully moved out of perceived orthodox positions during medieval times? Inquisition, torture, and even burning at the stake. In these days of consumer choice and religious pluralism, the idea of heresy might seem somewhat out of place. But I believe we need heretics today. What's more, I believe heresy can be a positive rather than a negative force in our spiritual journey. Of course, it can be argued that there is no orthodoxy today—no one way to practice religion anymore, and hence heresy no longer exists. Instead, individuals only adopt opinions or positions that suit them. But Peter Berger said it well in his book *The Heretical Imperative*:

> In the premodern situation there is a world of religious certainty, occasionally ruptured by heretical deviations. By contrast, the modern situation is a world of religious uncertainty, occasionally staved off by more or less precarious constructions of religious affirmation. . . . For premodern man heresy is a possibility— usually rather a remote one; for modern man, heresy typically becomes a necessity. Or again, modernity creates a new situation in which picking and choosing becomes an imperative.

Whereas the medieval heretic created ruptures in the existing order, contemporary heresy is a means to a new end, a way out of what no longer works. It can be a way forward. I believe that every age, and particularly an age like ours, needs heretics—people who will push past and beyond the accepted conventional wisdom of the dominant group and pull us across sacred fences that hold us back and keep us tied to perceived orthodoxies. For me, a heretic is a spiritual insurgent, one who rises up against the established order from the *inside*—one

I believe that every age, and particularly an age like ours, needs heretics.

who heralds a newer way, another option, a fresh view. A heretic either burns in flames or lights the way for a new generation.

Heresy has been with us a long time. The monotheism of Moses was new and heretical for his people. Buddhism was Hinduism's heresy, and Christianity was Judaism's. But since the 1960s, heresy has moved out of the exclusive realm of the religious and into the broader culture. Heresy and heretics are everywhere in today's business world. Institutions find new life by embracing heretical ideas. "Those who do not understand change are condemned to stay the same" would be the rallying cry of the heretical impulse in the twenty-first century. These individuals break the deadlock; more often than not, it takes a heretic or at least a heretical idea to challenge the status quo.

There are heretics in every organization. Our particular concern is the religious type, hence the title of this book. I will approach the idea of heresy from two angles. First, heresy as a means of dissent. I will show how heresy can be a way out of our present state of affairs. In doing so, I'll provide an interpretation of our current religious context and highlight some of the flaws of our present systems. Although I'll be candid with my critique, my intention is not to start a fight or pit one side against another. Instead, I simply want to speak from my own experiences and offer insight as appropriate.

It is worth noting at this point, too, that dissent is not disloyalty. The business guru Art Kleiner said that a "heretic is someone who sees a truth that contradicts the conventional wisdom of the institution—and remains loyal to both entities." This is how I see myself as I begin this endeavor.

Second, heresy also implies new thought. Using this angle, I will offer readers another way of looking at the issues I have raised and a new pathway to expressing their faith.

My intention is to look at life with God in the twenty-first century and to consider what Christian faith might have to offer. But I am not merely seeking to put a new spin on old beliefs; I am actually declaring that there are new ways of believing when it comes to the Christian story.

For those of you looking for a road map, you'll notice that the book is divided into three sections, and each section contains three chapters. The first chapter in each section will present the major subject matter, the second chapter will focus on my dissent, and the third will leave you with a new perspective to consider. The first section, "Questioning Grace," will explore what the new spiritual impulse in our time looks like. Drawing on a number of sources from theology to electronic pop music, I will look at the reasons why religion's day might be over.

> i am actually declaring that there are new ways of believing when it comes to the christian story.

The second section, "Questioning What We Know," will explore the deconstruction of institution-based faith expressions. Do we need church or temple anymore? Are there other ways to practice faith communally? Does any faith community have the power and the right to condemn, judge, and decide the destiny of others? I will also examine why religious institutions often become bastions of exclusivity and hatred rather than inclusivity and love.

The third and final section, "Living in Grace," will focus more tightly on the future and on the emergence of what I call "mystical responsibility," a new way of practicing faith in the world today. A concluding chapter will offer some thoughts on heresy as a way of life, keeping the conversation open and ongoing, and inviting you to begin your own heretical journey into eternity.

To reflect on religion is fraught with danger—this I readily admit. To mess with people's beliefs is a precarious venture, riddled with hazards. I acknowledge my own imperfections in these matters.

> it's worth exploring what the christian faith could look like if we . . . looked at the gospel story with twenty-first century eyes.

Nevertheless, I think it's worth exploring what the Christian faith could look like if we took some risks, pushed some tired old perspectives aside, and looked at the gospel story with twenty-first century eyes.

At this point in my life, I am happy to live with uncertainty and in precarious freedom, rather than hunker down in the false security of institutions and recite doctrines that no longer feed my soul. I have faith, and it is this faith that sustains me.

Asked where he would stand if he were excommunicated by the church, Martin Luther is said to have answered, "Under the sky."

INTERACT ONLINE

Join us online for an ongoing discussion about the ideas raised in this book. In each chapter, an interactive topic or question is posed to jump-start the dialogue. In our online forums, you can discuss your thoughts on the topic and see what others are saying. The Web site also allows you to submit and read articles, follow links, and find others in your local area to create discussion groups. Visit us at

www.spencerburke.com/heretic

SECTION I

questioning grace

the future of faith

I

Jesus Beyond christianity

I don't see Jesus Christ as being in
any part of a religion. Religion is the
Temple after God has left it.
—Bono, of U2

S itting in a prison cell awaiting execution for his part in an
attempt to assassinate Adolf Hitler, the theologian and pastor
Dietrich Bonhoeffer did what anyone in that situation might do. He
wrote letters to his friends and family. On April 30, 1944, the topic
on Bonhoeffer's heart was simply this: Does Christianity have a
future?

Titled "Religionless Christianity," his short letter pondered
whether the nineteen-hundred-year history of the church and its
theology might in fact be a preliminary stage for doing without religion altogether. It was a revolutionary idea all right, one that has
challenged Christians ever since its publication. Despite being
written more than sixty years ago, the letter's tone is remarkably
contemporary.

The letter is not the ranting of someone who has been hurt or
frustrated by religion. It is the heartfelt searching of a man who loves
God and wants his faith to matter. Toward that end, Bonhoeffer does
not advocate the abandonment of Christian faith as much as ask
where it is to go next. He questions, for instance, whether religion is

really necessary as a condition of salvation. Is it possible to encounter God's loving goodness outside the confines of religious patterns and practices? He also wonders why he so often feels drawn to be with people outside the church—the seemingly religionless—more than with those who share his faith. Further, why does it seem harder to talk about God with those who claim to know him than those who don't?

> is it possible to encounter god's loving goodness outside the confines of religious patterns and practices?

In the end, Bonhoeffer suggests that we have come to the end of religion as it has been traditionally understood. "The time when men could be told everything by means of words, whether theological or pious, is over," he writes, "and so is the time of inwardness and conscience, which is to say the time of religion as such."

Unfortunately, Bonhoeffer died before being able to elaborate on these thoughts, so one can only guess at what exactly he meant—or even the specific circumstances that caused him to reach these conclusions. Still, his letter does not seem to advocate abandoning the Christian faith as much as reimagining it.

I don't know about you, but I identify with Bonhoeffer's search—and many of his questions. I, too, think the time of traditional religion has passed. I've felt it in my own heart, and I see evidence of it in the broader culture as well.

To be honest, religion doesn't really work for me anymore. Being aligned with an institutional church or a particular system of worship seems increasingly irrelevant to my ongoing journey with God. In my experience, the customs, traditions, and even language of religion often seem to get in the way of honest dialogue about God. What's more, religion's airtight explanations and all-or-nothing theological arguments seem out of touch with the complexities of twenty-first-century life.

Though it's true that some people still seem to find comfort in religion's embrace, many more are exploring new interpretations of what it means to follow God. Obvious cracks are appearing in the foundation of traditional religion.

A fundamental fear

Religion, it seems, is no longer a source of cohesion in the world. In recent years, religious conflicts have escalated in frequency and scale. The stakes seem higher somehow, and the consequences more dire.

Since September 11, 2001, many commentators have talked about the "clash of civilizations," but I would suggest that what we're actually experiencing is a "clash of monotheisms." The zealots of the dominant monotheistic religions—Islam, Christianity, and Judaism—are at odds with each other and desiring dominance. Meanwhile, masses of the faithful stand on the sidelines in confused silence.

Driven by promises of paradise, some followers of Islam are willing to become suicide bombers. Driven by what they perceive to be moral conviction, some Christians are ready to bomb abortion clinics. While Islamists call for global jihads, Christians of a certain ilk call for an almost forced return of Christianity as the shaping force of American cultural life. They claim that the founders were intent on establishing this kind of society—conveniently forgetting that men like Thomas Paine and Thomas Jefferson opposed organized belief systems. In fact, Jefferson went so far as to inwardly swear "eternal hostility" toward organized religions.

Admittedly, all religions probably have a fringe element, but just the same, what is it about traditional religion that breeds dogmatic, sometimes fanatical, and even violent responses to the rest of

the world? Over the years, terrible things have been done and justified in the name of God. Just look at any history book. Is it any wonder the world's population is beginning to look for alternatives?
Frankly, fundamentalists of all kinds are scaring people off. The
more zealous and powerful these people become, the more potential followers they drive away.

Like it or not, religion is no longer regarded as a place to find
peace for the soul. Increasingly, sanctuaries have been turned into
war rooms. Perceiving the postmodern world as a threat to any concrete views of life and especially religion, fundamentalists and their
conservative cousins have become obsessed with holding their theological and cultural ground. In many ways, these efforts are like
putting a finger in the dyke, trying to hold back the sea of change
that ultimately cannot be stopped.

Writing in *Parabola* magazine, William Ventimiglia declares,
"Fundamentalism, in my view, is correct in wanting to preserve the
possibility of religious experience. However, it stands against the re-
lentless tide of conscious development in its efforts to confine individual religious experience to conservative organized expression."
He goes on to quote Jesus' analogy of the Holy Spirit as a wind that
blows where it chooses and writes that this element of God's action
in the world has "always been a problem for organized religion with
its well-established categories of understanding."

Fundamentalism, by definition, is an effort to protect the
fundamentals—or essentials—of the faith. The problem is determining just what those fundamentals are. In today's context, it
seems that fundamentalists are intent on hanging on to a particular
view of the divine that sacrifices the beauty of God's spirit and grace
in exchange for control and authority.

But what if Bonhoeffer was right? What if the last nineteen
hundred years of Christian theology and practice were just a temporary form of human self-expression? What if we have now reached
the point where we can live beyond religion? Could it be that we
will soon see the spirit released in the world in brand-new ways,

without the baggage of religion? Could it be that the eventual collapse of current religious systems will in fact prove to be a literal high-water mark in faith—that in fact many of the "fundamentals" aren't fundamental after all?

An Elusive Relationship

For years, preachers have appealed to people to join the church and experience Christian salvation using this phrase, "It's about relationship, not religion." The only problem is that it's seldom true. In actuality, the relationship promised by religion is usually predicated on commitment to the institution as much as it is to God. You don't have to be in a church for long to figure out what the expectations are—whether it's tithing, teaching Sunday school, praying, or going to confession—and what they expect you to believe becomes even more apparent.

Rather than facilitating a dialogue between followers and God, the church has a tendency to interpret individuals' relationships with God for them. Rather than responding to the call of God on their life directly, individuals often find themselves responding to the call of the church. What seems like obedience to the teachings of Christ is often adherence to external and dogmatic belief systems. This "false advertising" of sorts has no doubt also contributed to the interest in new spiritual paths.

We must also consider the claims to superiority that appear in virtually every religion. In Christianity, it is Peter who, in the

Rather than responding to the call of God on their life directly, individuals often find themselves responding to the call of the church.

book of Acts, declares emphatically to his peers and religious leaders, "Salvation is found in no one else [but Jesus], for there is no other name under heaven given to men by which we must be saved." In addition, most Christians also cite Jesus' own words in the gospel of John as proof of Christian superiority: "I am the way and the truth and the life. No one comes to the Father except through me."

These claims to superiority might not be problematic if they were a unique occurrence. But what happens when there are competing cultures in a world? Today, few societies have the option of living in "splendid isolation" anymore; the world is at once too big and too small. In this new pluralistic reality, we find ourselves dealing with competing claims of superiority.

Go to England, and you'll find a staggering number of religious television shows, not just Christian, but Islamic and Buddhist as well. All of them are quite similar in format, and each advances its faith as the true religion with varying degrees of intensity. What is a viewer to do?

In today's world, we no longer have just one religion seeking dominance but instead a cacophony of voices all vying for our allegiance. The evangelical preacher can be found next to the imam, who lives beside the Buddhist, who sits on an ecumenical council with the local rabbi. Each religion has different claims, and all are fighting for the hearts and minds of a searching global populace.

In addition, an unlimited number of spiritual and cultural perspectives are available to us through the Internet and satellite radio. These technologies make each religion's claims to ultimate truth even more difficult to resolve.

In the case of the Christian faith, one may be able to argue that the heaven and earth spoken of by Peter were not a literal heaven and earth. After all, back in biblical times, the world was thought to be flat, the earth below and heaven above. Likewise, when Paul speaks of the gospel being preached in all the world, it's conceivable that he may not have meant the Americas, Australasia, and any number of other places, since his "world" did not yet include these locations.

Even if one can somehow sort through these competing claims, the overall perception remains that organized religions propagate divisiveness. Of particular concern are groups who combine claims of superiority with power-based interpretations of foundational texts such as the Bible or the Koran. To say there is a deep mistrust of these groups in broader society would be an understatement.

But despite these problems, people don't seem to be rejecting God or turning away from the divine as they did in the twentieth century. Nor are they reducing the idea of the sacred to New Age generalities. Instead, they seem to be searching for new "religionless" ways to celebrate the sacred.

My own Experience

So what about me? Where do I fall on the spiritual spectrum? Frankly, I'm not quite sure how to answer that. Do I remain personally committed to Jesus and his teachings as found in the Bible? I do. I even think there's a place for great religious teaching and teachers. At the same time, however, I remain hopeful that faith can be practiced without the baggage of religion. I'll explore this idea throughout this book, but rest assured that the following pages will not simply try to convince you that all roads lead to God. Instead, this book is about a new way of looking at God and, in particular, the Christian message. I want to go beyond the religious categories that have governed the conversation so far.

The increasing interest in universalism among all but the most extreme elements of the world's religions suggests that an evolutionary shift is indeed taking place. For further evidence of this, one need only look to organizations like the Parliament of the

World's Religions or the proliferation of books by religious teachers highlighting the similarities between faiths. While I'm encouraged by this trend, I don't believe universalism is the complete answer. For me, it's the beginning of the story, not the end.

INTERACT ONLINE
Share Your Story

www.spencerburke.com/heretic/shareyourstory

A universal Longing

Universalism is basically the theory that all religions are inherently the same—that each of them is valid and can bring us to God.

As far back as the third century, Origen, one of the great theologians of the early church, affirmed the idea of universalism, saying, "The Word is more powerful than all the diseases of the soul, and he applies his remedies to each one according to the pleasure of God—for the name of God is to be invoked by all, so that all shall serve him with one consent." Even though his views were called into question by the church three centuries later and ultimately determined to be heretical, Origen attracted some high-profile supporters. Saint Vincent of Lérins said that he would rather be wrong with Origen than right with the world.

According to the *Oxford Dictionary of World Religions*, Muhammad is said to have declared, "If Allah is Allah, then there can only be what Allah is; there cannot be a God of Christians, a God of Jews."

Hans Kung, the great Catholic theologian, once wrote, "No survival without a world ethic. No world peace without peace be-

tween the religions. No peace between the religions without dialogue between the religions."

While these assertions sound promising, in practice, harmony
between faiths remains more dream than reality. So far it seems that
the world's religions aren't willing to engage in meaningful dialogue
with each other; and those who do represent a small and largely
unheard minority. Generally speaking, individuals who accept the
idea of universalism continue to live outside of the major religious
traditions.

While universalism bravely tries to resolve many of the conflicts and crises created by religion in our pluralistic world, it seems
a bit like that Coca-Cola ad from the 1970s. You know the one—
happy, smiling people from all over the world singing, "I'd like to
teach the world to sing in perfect harmony." If only it were so simple.

Unfortunately, the complex issues and difficulties of human
life cannot be solved with a Coke and a smile—either figuratively or
literally. In much of the Middle East, Coca-Cola has been rejected
and replaced with a new brand: Mecca-Cola. This product acknowledges the population's desire for a carbonated drink while at the
same time affirming the separateness of Middle Eastern culture.

The reality is that cultures and societies differ, and life is incredibly complicated. Sanitizing the religious landscape and removing all those differences does not resolve the tough issues. "Had
Allah willed He could have made you one community, but He hath
made you as you are," reads the Koran in chapter 5, verse 48. "So
vie with one another in good works. Unto Allah you will all return,
and He will inform you of that wherein you differ."

In this passage there seems to be something of the particular
as well as the universal. The idea is that all revelations are pathways
to salvation but different perspectives are necessary because of our
different cultural settings.

Nevertheless, there is still an obvious longing in the world
for some kind of resolution to the centuries-old conflict between

religions. At a recent concert in Los Angeles, Bono, lead singer of the band U2, theatrically put on a white blindfold inscribed with the word *coexist* during a performance of the song "Love, Peace, or Else." The word on his headband was made up of the symbols of the monotheistic faiths—the Christian cross, the Jewish star, and the Islamic crescent. The word was simultaneously flashed onto the digital light screens surrounding the stage. Through this powerful symbolism, it was obvious the band was issuing a passionate call to the audience to reflect on the need for peaceful coexistence in a troubled world.

In August 2005, the musician Moby posted an interesting journal entry on his Web site. Titled "Religion," the essay had a similar ring to Bonhoeffer's letter from sixty years ago. "So, do you think it's time to invent a new religion?" it began.

Because Moby has been up-front about his commitment to the teachings of Jesus throughout his career and frequently writes about Christ, on some level his actions aren't surprising. But at the same time, the fact that a rock musician would publicly explore the religious challenges of our time on his Web site does illustrate how often spiritual impulses are cropping up in culture—and not just in churches, mosques, and synagogues.

In his essay, Moby expresses concern with the ways society has changed over the years and how out of touch religion is with these new realities. In particular, Moby highlights the need for a new religion in light of the teachings of Jesus. For Moby, as for many people, the problem isn't Jesus; it's contemporary Christianity. Perhaps that's why he claims no religious affiliation. In his words, present-day Christianity is "depressingly Newtonian" in a world of quantum realities.

"Our human significance is both far greater and far smaller than anything that we've hitherto recognized . . . ," he writes. "We need a new way in which to look at ourselves and in which to understand our lives and our significance."

вeyond universalism

Bono and Moby are not the only ones calling for a new way. I recently spent some time at a local magazine stand and found all kinds of periodicals covering spirituality. From *Vanity Fair*, a mainstream periodical catering to the fashion and high-society types, to *Utne*, a compendium of articles from independent magazines from around the country, the media are regularly featuring articles exploring religion and spirituality as it unfolds in the twenty-first century. The articles tend to fall into two main categories: the continuing struggle to understand the rise of fundamentalism in the post-9/11 world and the new spiritual practices and ideas that are beginning to fill the marketplace.

Even among those who remain committed to traditional faiths, there are calls for new approaches to the practice of religion. Ziauddin Sardar, an Islamic scholar, notes that for almost a century now, scholars and thinkers have been calling for *itjihad*—reasoned struggle and a rethinking of Islam. In *Utne*, Parvez Ahmed, a board member for the Council on American-Islamic Relations, addresses common misconceptions about Islam and Muslims both inside and outside the faith.

Within the Christian tradition, there are a number of groups who also wish to reframe and reconfigure Christianity for the twenty-first century. Recognizing that the gap between church and culture is growing exponentially, they believe that continuing with the status quo will only assure the eventual demise of the Christian faith. While I agree with their assessment, I'm not sure attempting to make old beliefs fit in new packages is really the answer either.

For the most part, Christianity seems to be frozen in history—and recent history at that. When it comes to Scripture and its interpretation, modernity rules. Try as they might, most Christians today can't seem to get out of the quagmire of modern views regarding the role and function of religion. They may put a new label on the box, but the contents remain unchanged. For a society looking for alternative ways to practice faith, that's just not good enough. The product simply isn't compelling.

> The time is right for another way of looking at the christian message, freed from the confines of religion.

We need to move past religion. I believe the time is right for another way of looking at the Christian message, freed from the confines of religion and open to the possibility of a radical new incarnation and manifestation. The message of Jesus needs to evolve for our times.

In his extraordinary book *Stages of Faith*, James Fowler speaks of the development of the spiritual life as a movement through a series of stages. Using the analogy of moving through childhood to adulthood, he characterizes the various stages of faith and identifies what precipitates the movement to the next phase of the spiritual journey.

The second phase he terms "mythic-literal." This expression of faith, he contends, is characterized by its commitment to literal interpretations of beliefs and a linear approach to spirituality in general. The imagination is also curbed in favor of a more rigid structuring of one's world. That's certainly where I began my journey, and I know many of you likely did as well. The reality is that many people find themselves in this stage for a long time. Fowler says that what triggers the movement to the next phase is a clash or contradiction of stories. This clash inevitably leads to a questioning of one's values and perspectives. Previously held literalisms break down, and there is a disillusionment with teachers and teachings that once held us. The task then becomes the reframing of one's world by adopting a new relationship to it and breaking out of the mold that nurtured us.

Fowler's final category is called "universalizing faith." He notes that few people get here. It is the giddy realm where conceit breaks down and people transcend the categories that normally apply to the religious. It's where people transcend their own belief systems, if you will. Fowler called it the realm of the "subversives, the relevant irrelevants." I call it the *realm of the heretic*. It's where those looking for more than religious systems end up. It's where belief *about* God becomes participation in the sacred beyond religion.

> I call it the realm of the heretic. . . . It's where belief **about** god becomes participation in the sacred beyond religion.

who wants to be a heretic?

Copernicus and Galileo are among the world's most famous heretics. Both incurred the wrath of the church because they dared to challenge the prevailing wisdom of their times.

In a small work written in 1514, Copernicus introduced seven axioms about the order of the physical universe. Perhaps the most revolutionary and incendiary of the ideas was his declaration that the "earth's center is not the center of the universe." In fact, Copernicus was so afraid of being brought to trial on charges of heresy that he refrained from publishing the work until many years later. He died shortly after its publication in 1543.

It was Galileo's defense of Copernicus's theories that ultimately led to his own trial for heresy. In addition, Copernicus's book was placed on the list of banned materials—a ban, incidentally, that was not lifted by the Catholic Church until 1835. To the end, Galileo argued that Copernicus was right in spite of the accepted view of the day.

For years, people believed that the earth was the center of the universe. It had been the predominant view for so long that it became dogma. Eventually, an entire worldview formed around it. If the earth was the center of the universe, then the earth was the center of all worlds. And if the earth was the center of all worlds, then the church was at the center of all human affairs.

Before Copernicus, no one had considered that forces beyond the boundaries of the earth might sustain it. Copernicus proclaimed that the sun gave life and energy to the earth, not vice versa. But he didn't stop there. He went on to suggest that the earth was in a state of perpetual motion. Again, this was a radical idea. Medieval cosmology often depicted the earth as a static center with heaven above and earth below.

Not surprisingly, Copernicus had many detractors. Although he was personally committed to God and saw his work as a way of glorifying God, the powers that be were quick to tell him he was threatening the faith. Tolosani, a Dominican monk, wrote that Copernicus "seems to be unfamiliar with the Holy Scriptures since he contradicts some of its principles, not without risk to himself and to the readers of his book of straying from the faith."

What does Copernicus have to do with religion in today's context? A lot. For the bulk of world history, religion has been viewed as the center of all things—the "earth," if you will. Until recently, it didn't occur to anyone to look beyond it. Religion was the light that seemed to give energy to the divine impulses. Even now, it is hard for many people to think beyond the dominant idea that religion is the answer to society's need to experience the divine.

Throughout history, the church has put up creeds and doctrines to ensure that all things related to Jesus rotate around the axis of religion. The institutional church has become the center of the Christian universe. The challenge, I believe, is to reorder that universe. Jesus put it another way. Challenging the Pharisees on a point of law, he asked them whether the Sabbath was made for man or man for the Sabbath.

I believe that the next phase of faith is to move beyond religion. Nowhere does Jesus call his followers to start a religion. Jesus' invitation to his first disciples was to follow him. It was a call to journey, a process that leads us away from some things and toward others. It wasn't a call to adhere to a set of rules for all time. In fact, one of the most commonly heard critiques of the Christian message is that it is out of touch with what is really going on in the world around us.

> Nowhere does Jesus call his followers to start a religion. Jesus' invitation to his first disciples was to follow him.

"The purpose of theology," writes the theologian Sallie McFague, "is to make it possible for the gospel to be heard in our time." For the gospel to be heard in our time requires a commitment to spiritual growth and maturity. It involves being willing to break out of the boxes that have served us well in the past but no longer suffice today. While it's possible to preserve and pass on a centuries-old understanding of the nature of society, ethics, and even morality, we have to realize that these constructs are often powerless to speak into today's world.

Faithfulness to the message of Jesus does not mean that we must simply imitate our forbears in the Christian tradition. To do so might help preserve *their* formulas, but it will freeze *us* in history. I believe that we must attempt to recontextualize the story—to find equivalents for our world today. Jesus' message was a wake-up call to his people. In the Bible, in the second chapter of Mark, Jesus says, "No one sews a patch of unshrunk cloth on an old garment. If he does, the new piece will pull away from the old, making the tear worse. And no one pours new wine into old wineskins. If he does, the wine will burst the skins, and both the wine and the wineskins will be ruined. No, he pours new wine into new wineskins."

Here Jesus cautions the movement he is calling into being against appearing new or even progressive when it is in fact "old," meaning fundamentally connected to the dominant symbolic order. To do such a thing would jeopardize Jesus' vision of the kingdom of God. The old order was not sufficient to contain Jesus' radical message, and that is just as true today.

This tendency to hold on to the familiar remains a problem for many followers of God today. Religion becomes a place we retreat to, where we hear the old stories, lovingly preserved but frightfully disconnected from the realities of life. The rise of interest in fundamentalism is evidence of the desire for reassurance—for ways of fitting a complex world into manageable categories. But religions don't function at their highest and best when they attempt to provide simple answers to life's biggest questions.

The answer is not a retreat into the past. We must look instead at the "beliefs and ideas that stunt holiness today," as one writer put it. I believe we must resist our Israelite-like impulse to look back longingly at Egypt.

Undoubtedly, some people will see this call to reposition questions of faith beyond religion as dangerous and unscriptural. Many who come from a religious point of view may be threatened by the challenge to consider Jesus beyond religion. But as I see it, religion finds its gravity in the light of the sun. It finds sustainability and life through its relationship to the sun.

embracing the journey

As we enter this brave new world of the spirit, we can come with fear or arrogance or armed to the teeth with dogmatism. But that is not my desire. I venture into this world to conquer no one, to plant no flags and claim no territory, but to share what I hold dear from my tradition and offer my story about the grace of God as a gift to all who journey beyond religion.

Throughout this book, I want to explore what it means to move beyond religion—particularly Christianity. After all, that's the tradition I know best. But I believe that you will find value in these pages regardless of your spiritual background. I believe that the message of Jesus, once loosed from its religious confines, has the potential to contribute to the global yearning for the sacred and the divine. I believe that there is hope for the heretic, for God's grace is a much bigger gift than we've ever imagined.

what is a heretic?

There are five main types of heretics:

1. Church reformers—people who think the church needs to adjust its beliefs or practices beyond what the church is willing to do. For Martin Luther, this meant challenging the selling of indulgences and criticizing the role of the pope. Luther also translated the Bible into the vernacular so that everyone could understand it.
2. Eccentrics—individuals who usually work alone and hold fringe and sometimes bizarre beliefs.
3. Dualists—people who take the dualism of body and spirit to extremes. For example, the Cathars taught that this world is evil—even created by the devil, not God—and that pious Christians must separate and purify themselves from it.
4. Reactionaries—people who refuse to accept a new dogma of the church. For instance, when Vatican II proclaimed that Mass should be said in the vernacular rather than Latin in the 1960s, some people refused to change.

5. Intellectuals—includes scientific thinkers whose theories and ideas go against church belief, like Copernicus, who challenged the church's view that the earth was the center of the universe.

The church classified heretics in the following way:

1. The heretic impenitent and not relapsed (for the first time)
2. The heretic impenitent and relapsed (for the first time was penitent, now is impenitent)
3. The heretic penitent and relapsed (for the first time was penitent, now is penitent again, but relapsing was the capital offense)
4. The heretic negative (who denied his crime)
5. The heretic contumacious (who absconded)

Because the church doesn't thirst for blood (*ecclesia non sitit sanguinem*), the first four types were all delivered over to the secular state, which usually immediately punished heresy with a death sentence—the longest delay could be five days. Though not always observed, the custom was for the impenitent heretics (the first two types) to be cast into the flames alive; and the penitents (the third type) were first strangled or hanged and then burned.

Grace Beyond Religion

> The economy of undeserved grace has
> primacy over the economy of moral deserts.
>
> — Miroslav Volf

When my daughter, Grace, was born, she weighed just one pound, thirteen ounces. Twelve weeks premature, she was immediately put into the ICU.

With the doctors' assurance that Grace would pull through, I made sure my wife, Lisa, was comfortable, dealt with the necessary medical paperwork, and headed home to take care of our son, Alden. But I had barely arrived there when my phone rang. It was Lisa. "You have to come back to the hospital right now," she said frantically. "We have to say goodbye to Grace." In the time since I had left the hospital, Grace had coded. For forty-five minutes, doctors performed procedure after procedure, desperately working to save her life.

Lisa, who was still bedridden after surgery, was put into a wheelchair and taken to the neonatal intensive care unit. Little Grace, so small she would barely fill my palm, was almost invisible under all the wires and monitors helping to maintain her fragile hold on life. The nurses cleared the unit of other parents and left us alone with our baby to say goodbye. Our tiny daughter was not expected to last long. In fact, the doctor spent a long time explaining that due to her precarious health issues, it was merciful that she would not survive.

But after one hundred days of "living on the edge," Grace pulled through. She learned to eat, walk, talk, and play. Today, she's a healthy, normal five-year-old girl, dancing, playing dress-up, wrestling Daddy to the ground.

But what if this story had had a different ending? What if the worst-case scenario had happened and Grace hadn't survived? What would eternity have held for her? Would she have gone to heaven even though she wasn't baptized, had prayed no prayer, and had made no decision for Jesus or religion? What happens to babies and others who never get the chance to participate in religious life—or its redemptive practices?

Age of Accountability

Ask most Christians these questions, and you'll likely hear something about the "age of accountability." It's the idea that people who are unable to reason and make rational decisions for themselves are not subject to judgment. Instead, they automatically receive God's grace and go to heaven.

The exact moment, however, when this grace period ends and accountability begins is a matter of debate. Some religious groups believe that grace is assured only for babies, while others believe any child under the age of twelve is covered. The issue gets even more confusing when considering a precocious ten-year-old or an adult with a developmental disability. At what point does a person become responsible and aware of his or her actions?

Interestingly enough, the Bible is silent on the question. In fact, as far as I know, there is nothing written in the Bible specifically advocating an age of accountability. If anything, the concept seems to conflict with one of the church's key theological concepts: original sin.

The concept of original sin is often regarded as the backbone of Christian theology. Usually associated with Augustine, one of the great theologians of early Christian history, the doctrine proclaims that everyone is "born into sin." After all, according to Genesis, all human beings are descendents of Adam and Eve, the infamous couple cast out of the Garden of Eden.

The apostle Paul, writing in the New Testament book of Romans, declares that "sin entered the world through one man, and death through sin, and in this way death came to all men, because all sinned." He also says in his Letter to the Ephesians that we are all "by nature children of wrath."

It's that last part I find particularly troubling. Children of wrath? Wait a minute. I thought children were assured of grace until they reached the age of accountability. Things become even murkier if you throw part of Romans 10 into the mix. "If you confess with your mouth, 'Jesus is Lord,' and believe in your heart that God has raised him from the dead, you will be saved," writes Paul. "For it is with your heart that you believe and are justified, and it is with your mouth that you confess and are saved."

Baby Grace didn't confess with her mouth. Frankly, she couldn't do much of anything with her mouth for the first eighteen months. Even sucking was beyond her. We literally had to feed her through a tube in her stomach.

And yet if she had died, I can't think of anyone who would have said she wasn't bound for heaven. Somehow the idea of a baby going to hell just doesn't sit well with most people. Consequently, almost all religions seem to find a way around it. But they do it not by admitting that some things are simply a mystery but by adding to their religious systems. It's fascinating, actually, how far people will go to keep their religious systems intact.

INTERACT ONLINE
What issue started you to question your journey?

www.spencerburke.com/heretic/questionyourjourney

what exactly is religion?

Religion, at its most basic, provides a way of understanding the relationship between humans and the divine. But it's incomplete, so over time, elaborate systems, doctrines, and dogmas are developed to fill in the missing details. In fact, the desire to have our religions cover every aspect of human life is so strong that even when the sacred texts are silent, we'll find a way to make a connection.

Still, in spite of our best efforts, there are always things that arise outside the system—realities of life that don't fit neatly into the religious boxes we have made. "Concepts create idols," Gregory of Nyssa, in the fourth century, reportedly said. "Only wonder grasps anything." The complex systems we create with our religions may help us make sense of the world for a time, but eventually they outlive their usefulness. When life takes an unexpected turn or throws too many curve balls, these systems are revealed for what they are: finite attempts to capture the infinite.

The death of children has long been a problem for Christians. Could a good and loving God really send an infant to hell? Scripture doesn't seem to indicate otherwise, but at a heart level, it just doesn't seem right.

In the case of baby Grace, I believe she would have gone to heaven—but not because I subscribe to the age of accountability.

To me, the age of accountability is a loophole religious people have created to try and explain something that, frankly, can't be explained. They're so attached to the idea of original sin that the rest of life has to be oriented around it.

Again, to borrow from Copernicus, it seems we've got our planets in the wrong order. On some level, even the most die-hard chapter-and-verse types seem to sense that God's grace is bigger than religion, but they can't bear to let go of the idea that the earth is the center of the universe. The concept—religion—has become the idol.

consensual illusions

A consensual illusion is the way in which a society defines itself, both internally and externally. "American as apple pie" is part of the American common imagination. It speaks of who we agree that we are—down-home, friendly, family-oriented, and so on—and how we want to be perceived. It is what we are willing to accept about ourselves and the world around us.

Every culture has consensual illusions—things people assent to about themselves as a group, a people, or a nation. But consensual illusions are just that—illusions. They may not necessarily be true, or they may have been true at some time in the past. In any case, when the cover is ripped off or the curtain goes up and we see things as they really are, there is no going back.

Consensual illusions can be eroded in many ways. The Irish writer Thomas Cahill speaks of "hinges of history," seismic events that turn our world upside down. This can happen to us as individuals when life does not go as we think it should, but it can also happen to societies. There are times when it becomes obvious to the broader population that the illusion doesn't match reality. We say we are one thing, but in actual fact that's not who we are at all.

Many people have written about September 11, 2001, as a turning point in the American consensual illusion. In an instant, it became blatantly apparent that the United States was no longer impervious to external threats. "Why do they hate us?" Americans asked, trying to process the event. That day did much to erode our consensual illusion about ourselves and particularly about the world beyond our borders. But 9/11 is perhaps only the most recent event that has eroded our faith in our common imagination.

The events that marked the evolutionary shift from modernity to postmodernity were also hinges of history. Two world wars, for instance, did much to erode our faith in human progress and our belief that the world could become a better place through science alone. Similarly, 9/11 caused many people to view religion as a threat rather than a hope for the betterment of humanity.

Phyllis Tickle, author and thinker, has said that when events blow holes in our consensual illusions, religion is always a victim.

> When [something] happens, the first thing we pull out of religion, instinctively, is spirituality, and we reconfigure it. The next thing we worry about is the corporeality of the (religious) institution itself, and then the morality. And once we get all those things back in place, we have a new story, a new consensual illusion, and we're off and running again.

I agree with her for the most part, but I'm not sure I agree with that last sentence. As I see it, the three ingredients Tickle highlights as being in transition—spirituality, corporeality (the way we operate and organize our faith into religious institutions), and morality—are no longer dependent on a religious context for their future. Spirituality has been separated from religion in profound ways today, and frankly, I'm not sure there is any going back to religion anymore— at least not back to religion as it has long been understood.

A permanent Divorce?

Views toward religion in society have changed drastically over the years. Many people no longer seem to need a religious structure in order to practice their faith. Religion today functions as a sort of second-tier resource, providing tools, rituals, and concepts for those developing new ways of practicing faith. Nowadays, it's not uncommon to bump into people who will tell you they are Zen Buddhist Jews or techno-pagans or followers of Jesus who add a pinch of yoga, a dash of meditation, and a drop of goddess wisdom to their practices. I'm not saying that religion and religious institutions will disappear anytime soon, simply that our relationship to them has *already* changed.

Carter Phipps declared that the "new forms of spirituality that will likely emerge from the ongoing collision of the ancient, modern and postmodern worlds will be unlike any that this planet has ever seen before." He also said what some are less inclined to say openly—that the great religious traditions are "falling far behind the curve in today's global, pluralistic society."

> Religion today functions as a sort of second-tier resource, providing tools, rituals, and concepts for those developing new ways of practicing faith.

There are many reasons for this, but part of it is religion's unwillingness to change with the times. It's odd, really. For centuries, religion generally developed along the arc of human progress, but it no longer seems to be the case. At some point, religion dug in its heels and stopped advancing.

As I mentioned earlier, the dark side of religious history has left a sour taste in the mouths of many, and consequently, our society seems to view itself as largely postreligious. According to a recent poll, of the 33 percent of Americans who see themselves as "spiritual but not religious," nearly half view religion in a negative light.

For many people today, the divide between spirituality and religion is in fact permanent. There seems to be a growing sense that religion, as we have traditionally understood it, is no longer vital to the celebration of the sacred in our lives.

Personally, I'm eternally indebted to the great traditions for their commitment to preserve the sacred dimension of life throughout the ages. As I look at history, I can appreciate the role religions have played in human transformation, and it concerns me when these contributions are overlooked. To be sure, I've been nurtured and continue to be blessed by the richness of my own religious heritage. But I'd be lying if I didn't say that I've felt a definite shift in my heart. Times have changed, and religion just doesn't "work" the way it once did. The "hinges of history" have exposed this consensual illusion for what it is. At the end of the day, I see religion as a human construct—useful in some cultural contexts and potentially harmful in others.

At the end of the day, I see religion as a human construct—useful in some cultural contexts and potentially harmful in others.

Is it a good thing that religion is in decline? It's hard to say. The important thing, I think, is to realize that things will be different.

Consider the concept of family, for example. For centuries, we seemed to have a common understanding regarding family. The illusion revolved around what is usually called the nuclear family—

husband, wife, and kids. We understood the various gender roles. We knew who was supposed to do what. And in case there was any doubt about how things should be, those great television shows of the 1950s and early 1960s—*Leave It to Beaver* and particularly *Father Knows Best*—told us all we needed to know about how a family was supposed to work. But let's be honest. In real life, a patriarchal household wasn't always a recipe for domestic bliss—and a white picket fence didn't guarantee emotional health.

After the Second World War, of course, social dynamics changed. While it's true that the generation of women who strode off to the factories and aircraft hangars in the war effort returned to their prior roles when their men came home, this was not the case for their daughters and granddaughters. The landscape of the working world changed, and a new breed of woman emerged: the working woman, educated, competent, and no longer dependent on a man to provide for her.

Yes, something was lost in terms of male identity because of this change in society. But something else was gained. Over time, we saw a move toward gender equality in the workplace. Society began to put a greater value on women. Domestic abuse was no longer tolerated.

Today, the family portrait with the man as the dominant breadwinner is viewed alongside snapshots of other family structures. From the increasingly dominant single-parent family to gay, lesbian, and other alternative groupings, there is no longer only one universal family portrait. Is this a loss? Is society worse off because the traditional nuclear family no longer defines what a family is? If you're a child, is it better to live in a home with a single dad—or even two dads—who love you than with a mom and a dad who abuse you? Really, what's more important: that your family "fits" or that it functions?

Similarly, some people see the growing divide between religion and spirituality as a loss. They bemoan the shift away from religion and decry secularism because they cannot conceive of alternative ways of encountering God. But with the loss of religion comes the opportunity for other ways of practicing faith to emerge.

A Brief History of Religion

The majority of the great religions of the world all emerged in a period that the philosopher and historian Karl Jaspers has dubbed the Axial Age, the roughly thousand-year period from approximately 800 B.C. to A.D. 200. This time was pivotal to the development of human spirituality. From this rich bed of ideas and visions about the human relationship with the divine emerged what was later called, according to Jaspers, "reason and personality."

The religions of the first Axial Age made the world what it is today. They helped shape society and culture and were foundational to the development of the arts, trade, commerce, and other fields. This was also the period during which humans began to take responsibility for things previously projected onto the gods.

Without a doubt, at one point in history, religion was a revolutionary step forward for humanity. Its fingerprint and influence could be seen throughout society. But it seems that this is no longer the case. Institutional religion is no longer the only means or the most useful means of advancing ideas about faith.

Religion, it seems, works best in fixed societies—in cultures and contexts where ideas are static and boundaries are clearly defined. But this is not the postmodern world. Our world is transitional and ever evolving. Call it cynicism if you will, but we've seen through and detached ourselves from many of the things that have given shape and meaning to human life in previous generations.

As Phyllis Tickle has noted, the development of Alcoholics Anonymous (AA) probably did as much as other, more celebrated events to undermine our concept of religion. Emerging in the late 1930s, AA made it acceptable to talk about a generic God—"a higher power." Consequently, a generation of people began speaking about God in new ways not previously sanctioned by the consensual illusion—and traditional religious perspectives began to change as a result.

The change in attitude toward religion has also resulted in a new view of corporeality—or how we organize and operate our belief systems. One of the biggest trends in postmodern culture is an increasing suspicion toward institutions linked to modernity. Even though religions like Christianity trace their history far back before the dawn of modernity, many people view the institutional church today as a product of the failed modernist project.

The increasing pluralism that characterizes so much of life today has led to a different kind of relationship with organizations and institutions. Loyalty is manifested differently and is much more flexible and fluid. Even regular churchgoers are attending and engaging with institutions in vastly different ways than their forbears. Regular churchgoing is much more likely to be a monthly event than a weekly ritual, and "church-hopping" is at an all-time high. For many people, going to church is only one part of their spiritual life.

Other practices and rituals like AA or other support groups are also seen as contributions to the sum total of their spiritual lives. In addition, denominational affiliation no longer seems to be the deciding factor when it comes to choosing spiritual activities. Some people say we have moved into a postdenominational mode. Whether the sign out front says Lutheran, Methodist, Pentecostal, or Baptist seems increasingly less important; what matters is the church's ability to meet our spiritual needs.

As for Tickle's final ingredient, morality, we also find ourselves in a new and interesting time. Traditionally, the great religions have shaped the moral and ethical lives of cultures and individuals. Our understanding of morality was handed down to us from our gods—whether it was Moses delivering the Ten Commandments, Buddha advocating the fourfold path, or the philosophers hammering out ethics through debate.

Frankly, it's hard to understand the concept of morality out-side of a religious or philosophical framework. Our sense of right and wrong, and our views on marriage and sexuality, all came from the religious teachings passed on to us. As the theologian Elizabeth Debold has observed, "One's moral code was grounded in the belief system of one's culture, cementing the bonds of shared understand-ing within a particular community or group. . . . But in our increas-ingly postmodern age, the spiritual has become divided from the moral."

As we move away from the concept of religion's universal truths that apply to all peoples everywhere in favor of much more particular and contextualized views of life, morality is at the cross-roads. If religion no longer provides the moral framework, what will?

Contrary to popular opinion, I believe that spirituality is not just personal opinions about God and the divine. Indeed, the chal-lenge of moving beyond religion is to go beyond wallowing in some sort of postmodern spiritual nar-cissism. For me, this temptation is remedied by remaining deeply committed to the teachings of Jesus. Moving beyond religion does not mean we have to live in a moral vacuum of our own cre-ation. The fact is the world needs morality—perhaps now more than ever. What's more, there's a need for a global morality as well, es-pecially given the interconnect-edness of contemporary life.

> Moving beyond religion does not mean we have to live in a moral vacuum of our own creation.

Throughout history, religions have attempted to unify the world by seeking converts to their particular visions of the relation-ship between humanity and the divine. They've offered humanity a global vision of life's ultimate meaning as filtered through their teachings. But more often than not, these efforts have been perceived as attempts at dominance, making for an uneasy relationship with the world. Religion, it seems, is often about what makes us different and separates us, while spirituality seems to be more about what we can hold in common and what might connect us.

In the story of the woman at the well, Jesus entered an area that was technically off-limits to faithful Jews and began talking with a Samaritan woman. Jews particularly despised Samaritans because they dared to say that they too worshiped the God of Abraham, but on their own terms. So when Jesus allowed the woman to draw him some water, you can bet people noticed. It was a risky move in a religion based on purity codes. To take something from someone declared unclean by the rules and regulations of religion meant that you became unclean as well and therefore unable to access God. But Jesus wasn't put off by that fact. What's more, he went on to have a wide-ranging conversation with the woman about everything from the number of husbands she had to the specifics of true worship.

Religion, by nature, always tries to divide. "Our fathers worshiped on this mountain, but you claim that the place where we must worship is in Jerusalem," the woman pointed out to Jesus. He responded that where people worship doesn't really matter. What matters is that we worship in honesty and truth. "Believe me, woman," Jesus continued, "a time is coming when you will worship the Father neither on this mountain nor in Jerusalem. . . . A time is coming and has now come when the true worshipers will worship the Father in spirit and truth, for they are the kind of worshipers the Father seeks."

Spirituality seeks common ground. "All over the globe, people have been struggling with these new conditions and have been forced to reassess their religious traditions, which were designed for an entirely different type of society," writes Karen Armstrong. ". . . People are finding that in their dramatically transformed circumstances, the old forms of faith no longer work for them: they cannot provide the enlightenment and consolation that human beings seem to need."

That brings us back to baby Grace. As I mentioned earlier, the age of accountability seems to be an escape clause. It's something Christians have developed to get out of the theological hole we have dug for ourselves by presuming that God's primary occupation is the "hell and judgment" business. But what if we've got it wrong? What if God's primary occupation isn't punishment for sin?

A Nasty Little Secret

Truth be known, most Christians have conceived of a God who is less forgiving and less compassionate than they are. If we can see a tiny little baby and say it must be welcome in heaven, what does it say if God (or at least the God we've created) doesn't have a desire to show mercy and grace to the most fragile of us? Religion always wants to keep people out until they jump through some kind of hoop to prove they are in.

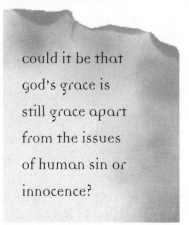

could it be that god's grace is still grace apart from the issues of human sin or innocence?

I think we've made a grave error in linking God's grace almost exclusively to the concept of sin. Christians say that grace is available only if people acknowledge that they are sinners. But could it be that God's grace is still grace apart from the issues of human sin or innocence—and there is no exchange economy to heaven?

Accountants and Brokers for Jesus

The gospel of Matthew includes the story of a group of workers hired to spend a day working in a man's vineyard. The workers agree on the wages they will be paid and quickly get to work. As the day progresses, however, the owner of the vineyard goes out into the marketplace, sees a group of men just standing around, and invites them to come work for him as well. He agrees to pay them "what is right." Later, the owner comes across still more men. He decides to hire them as well. This pattern continues throughout the day, right up until the last hour.

When the workday finally comes to an end, the owner of the vineyard tells his foreman to pay all the men, beginning with the ones who came to work last. To everyone's surprise, all the workers receive exactly the same amount. Naturally, the men hired first take issue with the man's generosity. "You have made them equal to us who have borne the burden of the work and the heat of the day," they say. To be honest, I think I probably would have complained as well.

The reality is that Jesus' story doesn't make economic sense. But I think that's the point. Grace doesn't make sense — economically or otherwise — and cannot be calculated like a day's pay. Grace is not about who is first or last, nor is it about adding things up into nice little packages. We really can't earn grace, no matter how hard we work; it is a gift from God. This was obviously something Jesus wanted to convey to those listening to his story.

The response of the vineyard owner to the disgruntled workers dramatically underscores Jesus' view of the economy of grace. "Friend, I am not being unfair to you," he said. "Didn't you agree to work for a denarius? Take your pay and go. I want to give the man who was hired last the same as I gave you. Don't I have the right to do what I want with my own money? Or are you envious because I am generous?" The man didn't cheat the men who worked all day out of anything by paying others the same wage even though they had not done as much work. They got what they were promised.

But what upset those first workers is what upsets all of us who get wrapped up in religious systems — the scandal of grace. I think we make a mistake when we start thinking that God somehow owes us something — or conversely, that no one else should get what we're getting.

Grace that is not vast and all-encompassing is not grace at all. Robert Farrar Capon, priest and author, said, "If the world could have been saved by good bookkeeping, it would have been saved by Moses, not Jesus."

Religion cannot fully contain concepts of grace because religion, in the end, is about bookkeeping. It's about maintaining balances of power. Consequently, religion can become a barrier that separates people from God. There comes a point when the religious system and all its demands keeps people out and prevents them from accessing what they need to find—God and, ultimately, salvation.

> There comes a point when the religious system . . . prevents people from accessing what they need to find—god and, ultimately, salvation.

Christianity sees itself as the broker between Jesus and the culture. "If you want to find Jesus," it declares, "you must come to church. Here we'll show you how to receive Jesus' gift of salvation." But the primary function of religion is not to be a mediator between God and humanity. In the Sermon on the Mount, Jesus says, "Blessed are the poor in spirit, for theirs is the kingdom of heaven." Who does the kingdom of God belong to? Not the priests and rulers of the temple system. Instead, Jesus forges a direct relationship between humanity and the kingdom.

The role of religion, then, is to point the way to God, not to control the flow. The goal is not to make people forever dependent on religion or the church for communion with God but rather to help them on their journey. Salvation is something that happens between God and people individually and has *communal* implications.

Rejecting Brand Religion

Karl Marx, the nineteenth-century developer of communism, had a low view of religion. Born into a Jewish family in a largely Catholic part of Germany, he was an avowed atheist for most of his life. His barb that religion is the "opiate of the masses" is familiar to most defenders of faith. What did he mean? Basically, that those in positions of power employ religion like a drug to dull the senses of those who have been marginalized.

Marx actually did little original thinking when it came to his views on religion. He derived most of his beliefs about the role of religion in society from the writings of Ludwig Feuerbach, whose influential book *The Essence of Christianity* was first published in 1841. Marx believed that Feuerbach had explained religion once and for all in his work and adopted his fellow German's theories into his own philosophical view.

Feuerbach believed that religion was a social production— simply put, a human invention rather than a divine intervention. God, argued Feuerbach, is the projection of humanity, and Christianity is nothing more than a form of "wish fulfillment." Like Marx, Feuerbach was an atheist and viewed his atheism as a means of liberating humanity from the concept of religion. Religion, as he saw it, encouraged dogmatism, intolerance, and arrogance.

There are few atheists left in the world these days, it seems. Over the years, more and more people have turned toward faith to find meaning and give shape to their lives. But interestingly enough, this rise in faith has not necessarily resulted in greater religious participation. Why? Because there is a growing sense that how we practice our faith is culturally and contextually defined. On this point, Marx and Feuerbach may have been right. Religion *is* a social production. What we know and understand of God does become the basis for the practice of our beliefs. Or to put it another way, our religions reflect our cultural understanding of what we think God is like. The problem with religion these days is that for many people, it simply no longer reflects the way they understand God.

John Drane recently published a book titled *Do Christians Know How to Be Spiritual?* It's a fascinating question, really. Like it or not, the wider cultural perception is that Christians have no connection with the spiritual needs of society. Drane's book suggests that the church needs to rethink how it organizes and operates if it is to again join the wider cultural conversation about God.

The British sociologist James Beckford tweaks Feuerbach's theory and describes religion as a cultural resource. In his view, religion not only carries the ancient truths but also offers symbols of new social realities—symbols that cover everything from gender issues to the environment. Religions, then, reflect the social realities of the cultures in which they emerge. Every religion has its own particular view of what God is like. Perhaps it is a name—Allah, Yahweh, Christ—or, like Buddhism's nirvana, a state of being.

These views about God or the divine are joined with historical accounts of each religion or sacred texts. From these sources come the rituals and practices religious followers must observe.

Christianity has a Trinitarian view of God. God is three-in-one: Father, Son, and Holy Spirit. Our image of God is male, and our faith is predominantly patriarchal. This, we say, is what God is like.

But even then, we are divided on what this truly means. The reality is that the Christian view of God has evolved over the centuries. In the Old Testament, God comes across as vengeful, angry, violent, and unapproachable. Moses, for example, has to hide his face in a rock to avoid looking into the face of God and dying. By the time Jesus appears on the scene, however, things have changed. Suddenly God is *abba*—"father"—suggesting that God is a compassionate and loving parent.

Islam, meanwhile, has ninety-nine names for Allah, each one invoking some aspect of his character. In the hills above Hong Kong, one can visit a place called the Temple of Ten Thousand

Buddhas. Built in 1949, the temple actually houses almost thirteen thousand statues of Buddha in all shapes and sizes, effectively allowing visitors to pick the Buddha that best reflects their own particular take on faith.

Not only do our views of God change as time progresses, but the way we practice our faith changes as well. We may place a high value on tradition and history, but the reality is that we are far removed from the situations and circumstances in which that faith originally emerged. I can study first-century Jewish culture all I want, but it's not the same thing as being there. And frankly, the information will always be colored, to some extent, by my current understanding of the nature of the self, human sexuality, politics, economics, and pretty much everything else.

Religious people love to think that their practice of faith is exactly as it was for those who worshiped centuries ago and that nothing has changed. After all, it can be an advantage to have the force of history behind you, lending you credibility. I think about two refrigerator magnets I saw once. "God said it. I believe it. That settles it," reads one, and right next to it, "Jesus Christ: The Same Yesterday, Today, and Forever."

But in religion, nothing ever stays exactly the same. Our religions are practiced within our cultural horizons, not outside of them. There is no such thing as a religion that exists outside of culture. Think about the way Christian missionaries in the eighteenth and nineteenth centuries evangelized the globe. They rode on the back of Western civilization and brought not only their stories of how God acts in the world but also the cultural contexts in which this God was to be experienced. For them, to be Christian was to be Western, which is why one can find Presbyterian churches in the deepest reaches of the Papua New Guinea jungle that look like they belong in the Scottish Highlands. It's also why most preachers in Africa today wear suits and ties to preach, even though their cultural dress is decidedly different. The poet William Blake said it this way:

This life's five windows of the soul
Distorts the heavens from pole to pole
And leads you to believe a lie
When you see with, not thro', the eye.

In the twenty-first century, Christianity reflects the culture it finds itself in—consumerist, materialist, and corporate. Zygmunt Bauman, a European sociologist, argues that the dynamic shift in Western society is best understood by recognizing that the idea of consumer freedom, not wage labor (which was the main shaping element of the modern world), is driving our cultural system. "I shop; therefore, I am," reads a poster created by the artist Barbara Kruger; it's a slogan that encapsulates our times. We shop for everything—not just staples and luxury goods but internal things like lifestyle and identity. "Consumption now affects the ways in which people build up, and maintain, a sense of who they are, of who they wish to be," observes the sociologist Robert Bocock.

Marketing Religion

In consumer culture, everything is a commodity, and everything must be packaged and branded, including religion. Consumer culture is all about choice. We shop to satisfy desire, not just meet needs.

I don't know about you, but my grandparents could tell some pretty incredible stories about less affluent times. During the Great Depression and the Second World War, all but the staples of life were totally unavailable—and even some of those were hard to come by. Today, it's hard to imagine a world in which anything you want isn't readily available. Just take a walk around your local market. Chances are you will find at least twenty-five varieties of each brand of spaghetti sauce—not including generics and house brands! You can purchase traditional, chunky, extrachunky, spicy, and organic versions of a wide variety of sauces.

I hate to be the bearer of bad news, but we don't *need* all those choices. They're available because we live in times of immense prosperity by history's standards. And this breadth of choice is reflected in pretty much every area of life. You want religion? There are plenty of options: New Age, Fundamentalist, Buddhist, Christian, Jewish, Pagan, Goddess, Zen, Hindu, Sikh, or any combination of these—traditional or spicy!

Choice is everywhere, and the only thing easing the pain of decision making is niche marketing and prepackaging. Good marketing and packaging lead us to make the choices we do. With enough research, planning, and design, a company can literally lead you to its products. But when it comes to marketing God, things get a bit more complicated.

Although the idea of marketing religion is an uncomfortable thought, religions have actually been doing this for centuries. As the author James Twitchell said, "If you like it, it is called saving souls; if you don't, it is called proselytizing." Either way, it depends on the tried-and-true concepts of marketing, branding, packaging, and distribution, which Twitchell claims were the invention of Western religion in the first place.

According to Twitchell, the Protestant reformers spent immense amounts of energy denying the holiness of many things that the Catholic church had infused with meaning. The removing of icons, the replacement of ornate crucifixes with empty crosses, the sacking of churches, and the demolition of monasteries were all ways in which they disempowered the Catholic church. They offered a repackaging, a rebranding of Christian faith, if you will, and infused the new brand with power by deconstructing the old.

In today's consumer culture, many of the traditional faiths seem tragically out of touch, and in a consumer economy, there is nothing worse than a brand that has lost its loyalty and credibility. Brandchannel.com claims to be the world's only online exchange about branding. On the site, advertisers and marketers from all over the globe discuss issues and share ideas.

In a rather uncanny sense of timing, the discussion topic on the site for September 2001 was "Does 'God' need a rebrand?" The conversation took a point-counterpoint approach and evaluated the brand in a variety of categories, including relevance, credibility, stretch, and differentiation. In the end, the site left readers to decide for themselves whether or not God met the requirements of a successful brand.

Although the tone may have been tongue-in-cheek, the subject matter was serious. On the relevance front, God was likened to the Oldsmobile—once a great brand but no longer a contender. Oldsmobile went out of business, and church attendance is down. Can the brand be revived—or is it time for a new model?

An interesting response to the questions came from Batsirai Chada, a creative director at an ad agency called SimpleClear. "The problem lies with the 'marketing staff,' not God. The church often misrepresents the brand, failing to communicate God's (the brand's) essence that in and of itself is quite relevant and impacting." In other words, the problem is religious systems, not God.

To some extent, the verdict on "brand religion" is already in. Consumers vote with their feet and their resources, and they are not buying what is being offered. Christianity, as the dominant brand of religion in the West for almost two thousand years, has lost its magnetism. According to the Barna Research Group, almost twenty million people have walked away from branded Christianity in the past five years. Their departure can no doubt be attributed at least in part to the way in which the story of God in Christianity has been packaged and presented to the marketplace.

Brand Christianity has basically reduced the relationship between God and humanity to a business transaction, while grace—the driving force of the Christian message—has become something available only to those who can overcome the obstacles in the packaging.

Brand Christianity has created its own subculture, complete with all kinds of trademarked goods. You think Life Savers are too worldly? Try Testamints. These "Christianized" peppermints come with a Bible verse on every pack, so you can testify with fresh breath—or as the Ship of Fools Web site says, "share the Good Chews."

Food, clothing, music, literature, movies, television, concerts, conferences, and festivals—everything these days is available in a Christian version. There is even a Web site devoted to Christian underwear! But the creation of this subculture has formed a gulf between church and culture and generated the perception of exclusivity.

Brand Christianity builds a wall around the church and a barrier against the culture. The "us versus them" mentality that results is a major obstacle to many people, and the message of Jesus has become so wrapped up in a particular package that its potential to engage all of society has been lost. Brand Christianity has turned grace into a commodity that can be accessed only through the embrace of a particular cultural form of religion, one that is increasingly unappealing to many seekers. In fact, it is increasingly appealing to a smaller and smaller niche market of consumers.

I am one of the founders of the Damah Film Festival, an annual gathering for short-film makers focused on spirituality. One of the festival entries in 2003 was a film called *White American Jesus*. The film is a comic portrayal of how Jesus is perceived by the church and those outside it. The title says it all, really. In America, Christianity is white, middle-class, and predominantly male. For everyone outside those categories, it's just not that interesting.

Rather than binding and gagging grace behind the walls of Christianity and making access to it conditional on the acceptance of culturally created ideas, I believe we need to present the message of Jesus outside of brand Christianity. We need to present grace in such as way as to generate genuine wonder and amazement.

Losses and Gains

It's not an easy task, and unfortunately, some people will see any attempt at a new approach to Christian faith as more loss than gain.

There will be losses, to be sure. For instance, there will be the loss of religion's exclusive claims on things like grace. But that claim was only a contextualized understanding of grace anyway. The important thing is that there will be gains as well. By letting go of some things, we can resurrect other key Christian ideas.

In the book of Genesis, God spoke to Abraham and proclaimed that his descendants would have something that would be a blessing to all the peoples of the world. Their designation as a "chosen people" was the way this gift for all of humanity was to be preserved. Christians took hold of this idea and today claim a special, and exclusive, relationship with God. Jesus called his followers the "light of the world." This has been interpreted to mean that Christianity has a unique place in the pantheon of world religions. The question, however, becomes whether or not we regard it as important that the peoples of the world call themselves Christian or that they benefit from the teachings of Christ, whether they embrace Christianity or not.

Maybe the greatest gift the Christian religion can offer the world right now is to remove itself from the battle for God. Perhaps it's time to release the claim to universal privilege it grants itself as the only "true religion." I realize that this may sound mad to some people, but I trust that others will be excited by the prospect of encountering the message of Jesus without the baggage of brand Christianity.

Increasingly, the conversation in our culture is turning away from religion and toward new interpretations of what it means to follow God. Whether it is in the pages of magazines like *What Is Enlightenment?* or in halls of academia, people are questioning the future of faith and pondering the demise of religion as a viable container. The Italian philosopher Gianni Vattimo has written:

> Christianity cannot realize its missionary vocation within the new order of relations among nations and different peoples and cultures by stressing its own doctrinal, moral, and disciplinary specificity. Instead, it can take part in a conflictual or comparative dialogue with other cultures and religions by appealing to its specific lay orientation. . . . This proposal could best be summed up with the slogan "from universality to hospitality."

Vattimo argues that the future of Christian faith does not lie in the realm of religion or brand Christianity. Instead, Christianity is at the heart of the shift toward secularity that marked the movement into the modern era. Rather than ignoring this or regarding it as the enemy of faith, he argues that the future of Christian faith lies in its ability to capitalize on the nonreligious dynamics of contemporary global society.

The stage is set

A secular society does not by default mean a godless society. It more accurately means a "religionless" one. The stage has been set for a new manifestation of the Christian story—a secular version—outside the confines and constraints of the religious realm. Not all the mechanisms are in place yet for helping people engage with Christian ideas about God and faith outside of Christianity, but they are beginning to develop. The cultural shift in favor of spirituality over religion and toward a God freed from the constraints of religious dogmatism and feudalism is exciting. The table is being set for the future, and I believe we will see the ideas that have captured humanity's imagination about God for centuries transitioned into new contexts.

Grace is bigger than any religion. Grace cannot be bound by any humanly constructed religion. Religion needs to embrace grace if it is to offer any hope to the world.

3

grace and the god factor

The spiritual landscape, rather than the
religious tradition, has become the arena
for theological exploration.

—Diarmuid Ó Murchú

One Sunday afternoon, I went down to the beach with my son, Alden. He was five years old at the time and just learning to swim. As we stood at the edge of the ocean, my son looked up at me and said, "Dad, do you know how much I love you?"

"No, how much?" I replied, caught off guard by the question.

"Well, if these waves were ten times taller than you and, like, forty times taller than me," he explained knowingly, "I'd take off this floatie and strap it on you. I would go to the bottom, but you would float to the top and be safe. That's how much I love you."

At first I was floored by his answer. It was such a profound comment for a little boy. And yet the more I thought about it, the more I realized that my son had touched on an issue with which I had been wrestling for a long time. How much does God truly love us? And perhaps even more important, what does it take to receive God's love?

Traditional answers always focus on some kind of transactional exchange—do this and you'll get that. The emphasis is on individual action. In the evangelical Christian tradition, you ask

Jesus to take your sins. How do you get the eternal life God promised? By actually praying a prayer of belief. You have to ask God to
save you. Fail to ask correctly—fail to pray the prayer—and you
might be out of luck. There are no free floaties.

But increasingly, these kinds of explanations minimize the
depth of the true love of God, a love that knows no bounds or limits. Could it be that God's love and grace are actually as subversive as my son's declaration of love to me that day? Could it be
that love finds us no matter where we are and we don't have to do
anything more to get it? Could it be that—beyond religion, reason,
and conventional wisdom—grace is something to be opted out of
rather than opted in to? Is it not something you get but something
you already have?

I'd like to think I'm the first one to explore this thought, but
I'm not. The idea—or at least the seed of it—has been picking up
momentum in our culture for some time now.

pop goes the spiritual

Nick Cave, one of pop music's most spiritually inclined performers,
sings these lines in "God's Hotel."

> Everybody got a room
> In God's hotel.
> Everybody got a room.
> Well you'll never see a sign hanging on the door
> Sayin' "No vacancies here anymore."

It is a musical sermon, advanced by the rhythm and refrain as much as by the substance of the message.

Ron Sexsmith has also explored this theme. In the opening line of his moving song "God Loves Everyone," Sexsmith asserts a subtle shift in perspective. He refers to God in the feminine rather than the masculine: "God loves everyone, like a mother loves her son, no strings at all, unconditional." Did you catch that? No strings, not even religious ones. But before dismissing his words as old-school universalism, take note of the next line: "Never one to judge, who'd never hold a grudge 'bout what's been done—God loves everyone." Sexsmith's idea of God transcends religion's attempts to make divine grace conditional. Free floaties for everyone.

For years, we have assumed organized religion is the only way humanity can have a relationship with the divine other—whoever that may be. But today, many people are beginning to realize that faith can exist outside the realm of organized religion. The only problem is that religious people don't understand this option—nor do they want to. They feel threatened by the shift to spirituality, and they're quick to point out its dangers rather than see its potential. Still, in spite of their best efforts, interest in spirituality is flourishing.

I know of a group of British friends, mostly people associated with the music business, who are trying to find balance in their lives after many years of excess. Although many of these men have a complete disdain for organized religion, they frequently talk about their spiritual experiences. They may not be religious, but they're definitely open to a relationship with a "higher power." It seems that the language of twelve-step groups has finally put God in loose enough categories to be palatable. Likewise, books like *The Celestine Prophecy* and *Conversations with God* have also somehow helped these men find connections with their spiritual lives when religion has only been a barrier.

The psychologist Carl Jung once said that it was absurd that people could think of themselves as having no religious side to their personality. In his opinion, it was akin to saying they were born without eyes. To Jung, people who declared a complete lack of religiosity had simply left that side of themselves in the unconscious. It's an interesting idea, but I think it's also fair to say that perhaps the necessary mechanisms just haven't been in place to help people see their spiritual side.

Religion has historically been presented as the *only* way the spiritual part of our humanity can be accessed. But what if religion is not the end of the journey of faith but the beginning? What if religion is only a step on the ladder to heaven and not the top rung? What if religion carries us only so far and cannot get us all the way to our destination?

what if religion carries us only so far and cannot get us all the way to our destination?

The Vietnamese teacher and monk Thich Nhat Hanh recounted the following tale in a recent issue of *Parabola* magazine:

> A merchant left his home every day, leaving his young son at home. One day thieves and pirates came and robbed the house and burned it. When the merchant came home, he found the charred body of a child in the ruins and believed that his beloved son had been killed. He cried and beat his chest. He reproached himself for having left the child alone. He cremated the body but was so attached to his child that he carried the bag containing his ashes everywhere he went. One day, a few months later, the child, who had been kidnapped by the pirates, not murdered, was released from captivity. He made his way back to his home and knocked on the door. "Father," he said, "I am back." But the father did not believe it. He believed his child was already dead. So he refused to open the door. And finally the child had to go away.

Hanh says this story, attributed to the Buddha himself, teaches that if we adopt some misconception as absolute truth, it will actually prevent us from ever truly reaching the truth. Even when truth comes knocking, we will not recognize it. The moral of the story, from Hanh's perspective, is that we should not get too attached to dogmatic views of how we think things should be. Sometimes what we think we know becomes an obstacle to the truth. This applies to the truths of our faiths as well as the faiths themselves.

sometimes what we think we know becomes an obstacle to the truth. This applies to the truths of our faiths as well as the faiths themselves.

One of the absolutes we have lived with for a long time is that religion is the best way to access and understand the sacred. But as the thirteenth-century mystic Meister Eckhart said, "Only those who dare to let go can dare to reenter."

While it's true that religion has given us a sense of the sacredness of life over the years, it's not the only option out there anymore—and certainly no longer the most attractive.

First, there is the growing perception of religion as a social production. This is not to say that divine revelations are necessarily human inventions. Many people still believe that God can reveal himself or herself. But the way this revelation is processed is increasingly regarded as a human effort rooted in cultural context.

Second, there is a growing awareness that religions of all kinds are prone to blindness and idolatry that can cause immense suffering to the world. From the ancient Crusades and recent terrorist acts to the Catholic Inquisition and Islamic jihads, many lives have been lost as a result of religious zeal. Similarly, many lives have also been lost because of religious apathy. In a world devastated by AIDS and poverty, the church has been largely silent and motionless. More and more people are moving away from religion because they can no longer tolerate violence—whether active or passive— done in the name of religion.

Third, our understanding of religion has changed. Today, religion is increasingly viewed as a part, and not the whole, of a meaningful spiritual life. Constant growth and adaptation are to be expected in life, and a quest for the sacred doesn't necessarily end in a church. People are exploring less trodden paths, with new expressions of the spiritual life challenging the reign of religion.

No doubt part of religion's demise can be seen as symptomatic of an increasingly postmodern culture. I hesitate to use the "p-word" because I really don't want to get into a struggle over what postmodernism is and isn't. But semantics aside, I think it's clear that the way people engage with and practice their faith, whatever it may be, is changing.

Generally speaking, objectivity is being replaced by subjectivity. People today often take their cues from their own internal life rather than external institutions. It's a shift from third-person living, whereby we see the bigger picture, to first-person living, whereby we view the world only from our own limited perspective. First-person living is characterized by a heightened sense of personal autonomy. It's the feeling that you are "your own person," fully able to take responsibility and make choices apart from the authority of any institution.

Our culture is also increasingly diverse. While it's true that pluralism has been with us a long time, in today's globally interconnected world, we're much more aware that there are multiple responses to life's questions and trials. Swearing up and down that there is only one single answer to any of life's issues seems naïve at best.

Democracy is also critically important in our culture. Democracy emphasizes respecting others' rights. It grants them personal liberty and freedom regarding their life choices. Accordingly, systems that seek to marginalize or isolate people, especially in the name of religion, are by and large rejected.

Interestingly enough, these postmodern themes also resonate in the message of Jesus. He democratizes grace, making it freely available to all people and challenges all who seek to prevent access to it. Jesus also calls those who uphold religious traditions to rethink the ways in which they mediate God's grace. He calls his followers to come in line with *his* take — not theirs — on the expansiveness of God's grace, rejecting any narrow religious characterization of it.

As we read the gospels, we see how the religious community at the time failed to respond to Jesus' call. The same may be true today. Despite the changing needs of humanity, religion seems unwilling to change and address the issues of the spirit.

> Despite the changing needs of humanity, religion seems unwilling to change and address the issues of the spirit.

Like it or not, religion is standing in the way of faith for many people. Chalk it up to the impact of fundamentalism or the constant moral rhetoric of religious leaders, but would-be seekers often feel judged before they even start their journey toward the sacred. Turn on the TV, and you'll find televangelists threatening communities with God's judgment because they reject school board members who support Creation. Flip to another channel, and you'll find religious leaders blaming natural disasters on God's wrath or on karma. As unbelievable as it sounds, a number of Christian Web sites viewed the tragedy of Hurricane Katrina in New Orleans as retribution for the city's support of gay parades. Ironically, the area where those parades are held was the only part of the city that survived virtually unscathed! As Steven Colbert of *The Daily Show* noted, it was the "gay-adjacent areas that seemed to be hardest hit!" Oddly enough, even the Dalai Lama seemed to suggest to Larry King that karma might have played a role in the tragedy. No wonder people often have a bad taste in their mouth when it comes to religion.

In contrast, spirituality—the movement beyond religion—is characterized by a desire to move past judgment and other characteristics that have typically defined religion. It seeks to find new ways to express the sacred in our lives.

In their book *The Spirituality Revolution: Why Religion Is Giving Way to Spirituality*, authors Paul Heelas and Linda Woodhead write:

> The expectation would be that in the West those forms of religion that tell their followers to live their lives in conformity with external principles to the neglect of their unique subjective-lives will be in decline. . . . By contrast, those forms of spirituality in the West that help people to live in accordance with the deepest, sacred dimensions of their own unique lives can be expected to be growing.

spirituality 101

So just how does spirituality compare with religion? Here's a quick summary of the differences—at least as I see them.

- Spirituality encourages us to treat each human being equally and to explore the feminine of the divine as well the masculine. Religion, conversely, is dominated by male imagery and in many places continues to oppress and undermine women. The patriarchal nature of most of the world's religions often means that women have to fight for the right to be treated equally.

- Spirituality encourages a countercultural dynamic. It challenges many of the values of material life by injecting a renewed focus on the divine. On the other hand, religion and the establishment tend to go hand in hand. While the sacred texts may encourage countercultural living, in practice, religion has embraced the values of contemporary life.

- Spirituality trades in mystery and seeks experiential, firsthand encounters of the divine. Religion, meanwhile, frequently comes across as overly dogmatic and absolutist. Religion too often imposes blanket rules and regulations on us without considering context or social and environmental dynamics.

- Spirituality is concerned with conscious living and with cultivating the sense of interconnectedness. Religion, by comparison, is often held captive by pseudo-orthodoxy and tends to be concerned with professions of belief rather than transformational living.

- Spirituality adopts a "both-and" approach to life, allowing culture, context, and situation to be reflected in the beliefs and practices of the seeker. Whereas spirituality encourages tolerance and the acceptance of difference as the foundation for postmodern ethics, religion tends to trade in binary oppositions. It is most comfortable with clear boundaries and "us and them" divides.

- Spirituality seeks to move beyond the authority structures that have dominated organized religion, instead ascribing authority to each individual. Religion, on the other hand, confers authority to a select few in leadership. It tends to be hierarchical and exclusive.

- Spirituality favors a holistic view of the individual, seeing the self not as a series of compartments but as a whole entity. The tendency of religion, meanwhile, is to divide body and spirit, emphasizing the spirit's superiority over the body.

- Spirituality is concerned with the particular rather than the universal. It holds that the subjective-self narrative is integral to the expression of authentic faith. Religion, in contrast, is consumed with accounts of the universal human condition. As a result, people reject religion not because they don't believe but because their individual stories are overlooked and their voices aren't heard.

- Spirituality is material (meaning of *this* world) and tries to connect the world of the divine with the world of the human. Religion, on the other hand, is external and generally focused on "otherworldly" experiences. It often has very little to say about the sacredness of all creation here and now.

- Spirituality focuses on authenticity and honesty. Religion tends to emphasize perfection and holiness. In fact, so great is the pressure to be progressing that people often lie to each other and even themselves about their religious experience and where they really are in their lives.

- Spirituality operates on a new cosmology that sees a "multiverse" rather than the universe. It attempts to redefine the practice and experience of faith in a post-Newtonian world. As Marshall McLuhan said, "The phrase 'God is dead' applies aptly, correctly, validly to the Newtonian universe which is dead. The ground rule of that universe, upon which so much of our Western world is built, has dissolved." Religion operates on premodern views of the world. Ever since man took pictures of the earth from the moon, our understanding about cosmology and the nature of being has evolved into a postmetaphysical understanding of life.

- Spirituality begins its discussion of the sacred from the desire for an integrated life. Religions often operate on a sin-redemption paradigm, which has little resonance in today's society.

- Spirituality seeks to advance a communal and holistic celebration of the sacred and eradicate boundaries. Religion has followed an imperialistic and colonizing strategy, sacrificing the colorful texture of multiple perspectives.

To be sure, religion has been a great gift to humanity, preserving and disseminating concepts about the sacred down through the ages. But our culture is moving in different directions these days. The postmodern dynamics at work in our world are creating new understandings of what it means to be human and how faith and belief might be practiced and experienced. Sadly, the gatekeepers of many institutional faiths don't have much interest in pursuing paths that could bridge the gap between religion and spirituality.

INTERACT ONLINE
What would your list look like?

www.spencerburke.com/heretic/yourlist

Grace, sin, and spirituality

It's impossible to talk about the rise of spirituality without also talking about grace. Indeed, as I see it, grace ushers in spirituality.

What is grace? For me, it is a subversive and scandalous twist in human history—an unexpected and revolutionary turn of events that offered a new way of relating to the sacred and each other. Religion declares that we are separated from God, that we are "outsiders." Grace tells us the opposite; we are already in unless we want to be out.

This is the real scandal of Jesus. His message eradicated the need for religion. It may come as a surprise, but Jesus has never been in the religion business. He's in the business of grace, and grace tells us there is nothing we need to do to find relationship with the divine. The relationship is already there; we only need to nurture it.

> This is the real scandal of Jesus. His message eradicated the need for religion.

Of course, growing up, I had a much different concept of grace. I grew up in an environment where grace was described as "unmerited favor." The only problem was that getting this "unmerited favor" still required doing something—namely, "asking Jesus in your heart" or praying a prayer.

I'm reminded of those people in the mall who are always offering me a "free" gift—and then telling me I just have to fill out a survey or apply for a credit card to get it. Let's be clear. If I have to do something to get it, it's not free. The amount of effort I need to put in might be minimal relative to the value or size of the prize, but it's still effort. The offer is still predicated on some kind of transaction.

If grace really is unmerited favor and I really can do *nothing* to get it, then that should be the end of the story. But in my experience, it never is. Religious people love fine print. They just can't seem to get away from it no matter how hard they try. It's always "God loves you—but . . ."

The problem, I think, at least in the Christian tradition, is that grace seems to have no meaning apart from sin. The two concepts are always linked. It's not that I think sin is a myth or that everyone is perfect; it's just that I believe linking grace to sin detracts from its beauty and intensity.

Paul Tillich, a towering figure in twentieth-century Christian theology, had a lot to say about grace. In one of his sermons, he said:

> Grace strikes us when we are in great pain and restlessness.
> It strikes us when we walk through the dark valley of a meaning-
> less and empty life. It strikes us when our disgust for our own
> being, our indifference, our weakness, our hostility, and our lack
> of direction and composure have become intolerable to us. It
> strikes us when, year after year, the longed-for perfection of life
> does not appear, when the old compulsions reign within us as
> they have for decades. . . . Sometimes at that moment a wave of
> light breaks into your darkness, and it is as though a voice were
> saying: "You are accepted. You are accepted by that which is

greater than you, and the name of which you do not know." . . .
Simply accept that you are accepted! If that happens, we experience grace. After such an experience we may not be better than
before, and we may not believe more than before. But everything
is transformed . . . and nothing is demanded of this experience,
no religious or moral or intellectual presupposition, nothing but
acceptance.

As Tillich described it, grace is a transforming experience
that may allow us to begin the journey toward a more holistic and
integrated life, but it's not directly linked to any religious ideology.
It's not conditional on recognizing or renouncing sin, and it comes
to us whether or not we ask for it. We don't have to do something to
receive it, nor do we even have to respond to it in some way. It simply comes.

How it works, in fact, remains something of a mystery. The
Christian writer Philip Yancey reinterpreted E. B. White's comment
on humor to encapsulate his own reluctance to get too technical
when describing grace. Grace, he wrote, "can be dissected, as a frog
can, but the thing dies in the process, and the innards are discouraging to any but the pure scientific mind."

Nevertheless, many Christians are uncomfortable with mys-
tery. Their tendency is to dot every *i* and cross every *t*. Religious people want to know *why*. No doubt sin was initially linked to grace in
an effort to try to understand God better. In the years since, of
course, the idea has taken on a life of its own. Rather than being a
theory about how God may or may not work, it's become a central
tenet of Christian theology. But it's a problematic association.

Douglas John Hall has said there is no word in the vocabulary of Christians so badly understood in the world and in the
churches as the word *sin*. He spoke about the reduction of the concept of sin to "moral misdemeanors and guilty thoughts, words, and
deeds, especially of the sexual variety, that can be listed and confessed and absolved." Hall claimed that this reduction alone is part

of the reason Christianity has declined in the West. The concept of sin is meant to address the quality of our relationships, with each other and with the world in which we live, but the church has turned it into a "petty moralism that no longer speaks to . . . human persons in their complex intermingling."

Alan Mann, in his book *Atonement for a "Sinless" Society*, says that in the culture outside of the church, sin is understood "solely as an offence against a divinely instituted law—because this is the only story people hear from the church itself: we are bad people because we do bad things."

In a review of *The Chronicles of Narnia: The Lion, the Witch, and the Wardrobe*, the movie based on the writings of C. S. Lewis, the journalist Polly Toynbee writes, "Of all the elements of Christianity, the most repugnant is the notion of the Christ who took our sins upon himself and sacrificed his body in agony to save our souls. Did we ask him to?"

> Although the link between grace and sin has driven christianity for centuries, it just doesn't resonate in our culture anymore. It repulses rather than attracts.

Although the link between grace and sin has driven Christianity for centuries, it just doesn't resonate in our culture anymore. It repulses rather than attracts. People are becoming much less inclined to acknowledge themselves as "sinners in need of a Savior." It's not that people view themselves as perfect; it's that the language they use to describe themselves has changed. "Broken," "fragmented," and "lacking wholeness"—these are some of the new ways people describe their spiritual need. What resonates is a sense of disconnection. Sin would perhaps be better understood in our culture if it were presented as pursuing self-interest at the expense of the well-being of the larger (or smaller) horizons of our existence, whether through self-abuse or through lack of concern for the world in which we live.

Instead, sin has often been presented as a violation of the rules and regulations of religion. In Christianity, Jesus is held up as the model of sinless living, the ultimate example to which all humanity should aspire. "Jesus," it is said, "was tempted in all points as we are yet was without sin." This concept of Jesus as a sinless individual permeates Christian theology. But was Jesus really sinless? He certainly seems to have violated a number of the rules and interpretations of the Law that his contemporaries regarded as huge sins. He violated the Sabbath and excused his disciples for their violations. He interpreted the meaning of the Sabbath by telling the story of King David's questionable use of the Law in order to feed his men. He repeatedly talked to the unclean, the unlovely, and the unrepentant.

As I see it, Jesus may not have sinned against God, but he certainly committed sins against the religion of his day. Jesus lived his sinless life in grace—and that grace often transgressed the moral codes of religion. The challenge for followers of Jesus is to reframe the story and offer society a new understanding of exactly what grace is and what it means for us all.

converted—but to what?

People who encounter grace experience some kind of conversion. "By grace you are saved, through faith, and that is not of yourselves; it is the gift of God," Paul said in his Letter to the Ephesians. What does it mean to be saved by grace? Traditionally, this has meant that the individual has experienced a conversion to religion. Grace has been seen as a device that converts people to religion rather than a free floatie given in absolute, unconditional love.

I believe that grace is much more than that. In fact, I think it is quite possible to be religious and have no concept of grace at all. We have all probably run into those "holier than thou" religious people whose lives are marked more by judgment and criticism than by graciousness. Christians have reduced the grace encounter to the recitation of the "Sinner's Prayer"—a prayer, by the way, that you won't find anywhere in the Bible but is widely regarded as the way conversion begins. Repentant sinners acknowledge that Christ died for their sins on the cross at Calvary, providing salvation for all through his sacrifice. The assumption is that once people repeat this prayer, they are born again and will go to heaven when they die.

It is a lovely idea, but once again, it reduces the human-divine relationship to a onetime transaction rather than a lifetime journey. More often than not, the whole idea of salvation from a Christian perspective is linked to future time and space. "If you should die tonight, do you know that you would go to heaven?" pastors ask. It's a commonly heard encapsulation of the call to salvation. Why should you be "saved"? So you'll know where you will "spend eternity."

But to relegate the idea of salvation to the realm of time and space is to strip this important idea of its transformative power. All too often, religion teaches that information and knowledge equal salvation, but I don't think it works that way. Salvation involves faith, not belief. We don't experience salvation because we believe right things but because we have faith in the experience of grace.

> salvation involves
> faith, not belief.
> we don't experience
> salvation because
> we believe right
> things but because
> we have faith in
> the experience
> of grace.

Salvation and conversion are two closely connected ideas. Salvation is more than a transaction; it is an awareness that comes in a variety of ways, unique to each individual. Michael Dowd put it this way:

> To know the joy of reconciling when I've been estranged; to experience the ecstasy of forgiveness when I've been bound by guilt; to feel passion and energy when I've been sick; to see clearly when I have been spiritually blind; to be comforted when I've been grieving; to be empowered when I've been paralyzed with fear; to be inspired when I've been depressed; to let go when I've been attached; to accept the truth when I've been in denial; to be back on purpose when I've been floundering—each of these is a precious face of salvation. And salvation belongs to God, not to any religion; it is what God offers to all His children.

Conversion is a necessary part of salvation—vital, in fact, for our future. It is what connects us to the idea of salvation. But to what are we converted? Religion? No. We need to be converted to a fresh understanding of God's desire and vision for us. It's our perspective that needs to change, not God's. Eternity really isn't the issue. We need to see the vision of a life in God that Jesus brings.

we need to be converted to a fresh understanding of god's desire and vision for us.

So many times the stories of Jesus' encounters with people in the gospel are simply tales of how he reconnects them with God after religion has denied them access. They were rejected because they didn't fit the categories, either through their own folly or the outside forces at work in their lives, including sickness and crime. This is how grace works. Jesus opens our eyes to the truth about ourselves and the world around us. Thomas Merton spoke of the many conversions that lead to salvation as "epiphanies." Others call them "eureka" moments or "aha" moments—those times in life when we encounter something that makes our understanding of the world bigger and exposes our narrow views for what they are.

In Matthew's parable of the mustard seed, Jesus describes the kingdom of God as a mustard seed—the tiniest of all seeds. But when it is planted in the ground, it grows into a tree so large that its branches offer shade for the birds. Writing about this illustration of the kingdom of God, the German theologian Joachim Jeremias says, "Out of the most insignificant beginnings, invisible to the human eye, God creates God's mighty Kingdom, which embraces all the peoples of the world."

"All the peoples of the world" describes the Gentiles, people from different national and ethnic backgrounds, and others who were excluded from the Jewish religion. Like most religions, Judaism functioned as a gatekeeper in Jesus' time. It was primarily concerned with making sure no one slipped through without meeting the necessary requirements it claimed were part of God's revelation to them. That's why Jesus was perceived as such a threat. Jesus declared that as far as God was concerned, there were no outsiders, no Gentiles, no people or groups excluded from access to the "shade of God's tree."

My daughter, Grace, with her premature birth now five years behind her, loves to have me play "her" song. "Grace," by U2, is not just about her name. It's about her life. And ours.

"Grace," Bono says, is a familiar girl's name, but it is also something else, something truly radical. It's a "thought that has changed the world." The song explores the beauty and mystery of this thought, this grace, which has truly changed everything. In the band's view, the idea of grace is an antidote to the concept of karma.

Although the concept of karma has its roots in Hindu and Buddhist teaching, the essence of it—that a law of causality governs the universe—is common to most religions. For many people, I think the idea of karma, basically understood in the West as "you reap what you sow," is how they think that the universe and God work. You do right, and you get blessing. You do wrong, and you suffer the consequence. Karma has been integrated into our cultural vernacular to such a degree that we pretty much all know what it implies regardless of our religious affiliation.

Of course, there is much to be said for this idea, and I agree to a point. But as Bono points out in this song, grace introduces another way of viewing the universe. Grace "travels outside of karma," he sings. Grace interrupts this cause-and-effect view of life. If karma holds you to account for your errors and mistakes, your "sins," grace does not. Instead, grace breaks into this cycle and declares that our actions, good or bad, are not the determining factor in our relationship with God. Grace, not our religious practices, connects us to the divine.

The recurring theme in "Grace" seems to be that, in spite of the many mistakes we make, grace continually offers us hope, and a way out of our cause and effect religions. Grace heals our wounds, wipes away the bad marks against us, and makes the ugly beautiful. The last line of the song sums it up. Grace "finds beauty in everything."

I see grace as a connecting conduit. It's the gift that connects us with God. It has the power to move us away from checklist living, away from jumping through hoops and all the other ways religion makes us perform in order to receive its blessing. Grace is offered to all people, everywhere, regardless of religious affiliation.

It's difficult for any religion to mediate the richness and breadth of this grace. This is why I believe that it is grace itself that ushers in spirituality. The grace of God is too much for any religious group to have absolute control over. For when grace is forced into the service of a particular interpretation of the divine, something of its life is muted. A kind of counterfeit grace emerges. This grace depends on our own initiative. We may be literally drowning, but this grace demands that we dogpaddle to get it.

SECTION II

questioning what we know

new Horizons of faith

The End of the world as we Know it

The original cynics were a dusty group of
people who questioned ethics, not because
they hated ethics but because they loved ethics
so much. They questioned God and religion,
not because they were skeptical but because
they were obsessed with God and religion.
Questioning God is not questioning God but
only questioning "God"—in other words,
our understanding of God.

—Pete Rollins, founder of the
Ikon community, Belfast, Ireland

I must confess that I find megachurches incredibly fascinating.
From the huge parking lots, complete with shuttle buses and lot
attendants, to the six-thousand-seat sanctuaries, waterfalls, and bas-
ketball courts, these modern cathedrals are pretty hard to ignore. I
think part of my fascination lies in contemplating the future of these
buildings. I've always wondered what might happen to these behe-
moth structures if religious institutions lose their place in our culture. Will we one day take tram tours around the megachurch
campus at Saddleback in Orange County or Willow Creek in sub-
urban Chicago the way people tour the great cathedrals in Europe?

I mean, if it's true that grace really is bigger than religion,
what then? What lies ahead for the institutional church—particularly the Christian church? I'm not trying to be sensationalistic here

or paint some kind of *Left Behind* scenario. I'm simply asking the question.

In the United Kingdom, fewer than 1 percent of people between the ages of eighteen and thirty-five attend church services. Callum Brown has said that the "culture of Christianity has gone in the Britain of the new millennium. Britain is showing the world how religion as we have known it can die." In the United States, the situation isn't quite as bleak, but given that the average age of a church attendee is about twenty-five years older than the average age of the rest of the population, it's hardly a picture of health.

In Section One, I outlined the shift in the way religions of all kinds are perceived around the world. Now I want to focus on churches specifically. Is there a future for the Christian church as an institution?

Reality check

To be sure, the institutional church has weathered many storms before—most notably the Protestant Reformation of the sixteenth century. But the world at the end of the modern age seems planets away from the world of Martin Luther.

Ours is a world of global communication and interconnectedness. Whereas Luther had the printing press to help move his message forward, we also have the telephone, radio, television, photocopiers, fax machines, cell phones, satellites, Internet, e-mail, instant messaging, blogs, and so many other options.

Each of these technologies allows people to access more information from wider sources and to interact with more people around the globe. "New technologies of perception and communication open up new spaces," says Erik Davis in his book *TechGnosis,* and these new perceptions "thus unfold a new world, or at least new dimensions of universal nature."

The new information age of the twenty-first century has unfolded a new world that is everything the old one was not—multinational, multicultural, multidisciplined, and multifaith. This is the world in which the institutional church now finds itself.

"Man seems to have started from scratch four times," wrote the German philosopher Karl Jaspers, "with the Neolithic age, with the earliest civilizations, with the emergence of the great empires, and with modernity."

Phyllis Tickle argues that religion in the modern era, in Western society at least, can be book-ended by Martin Luther and the Episcopal bishop John Shelby Spong. Tickle also outlines some of the key social developments that have had a significant impact on religion.

1859—Charles Darwin publishes *On the Origin of Species*, which signals the end of religion or the beginning of a new incarnation, depending on how one feels about the theory of evolution.

1902—Albert Einstein, with his theory of relativity, introduces the idea of a fourth dimension, altering our concepts of time and space and leading to the post-Newtonian age of science.

1906—Albert Schweitzer publicly raises the question of the historicity of Jesus for the first time.

1909—The Azusa Street Revival marks the dawn of Pentecostal and charismatic Christianity.

1935—Alcoholics Anonymous begins the self-help movement and, more important, the opportunity to talk about a "generic" God.

1943—Sulfa drugs, penicillin, and other advances in medicine reframe human vulnerability (before these drugs, little but prayer stood between a sick person and death).

1945—The atomic bomb brings the dawn of the nuclear age.

1941–1945—"Rosie the Riveter" becomes an icon as women enter the workforce en masse to support the war effort, thus sowing the seeds of the female liberation movement.

1962—Birth control pills level the gender playing field, physiologi-
cally and psychologically.

1969—Pop culture opens the door to Asia, and throngs of young
people already disenfranchised from Christianity embrace
the East and Buddhism.

1969—The drug age introduces the chemically induced self and
adds to the destabilization of the self already occurring with
other changes in social orientation.

Even if we stop there, it is easy to see how these changes have
posed a challenge to the traditional authority and answers of the
institutional church. If we think of events in more recent years and
add in the way technology has transformed the ways we communicate and interact, the idea of living in a pivotal moment in human
development becomes even clearer. In fact, it seems that we are entering into a fifth Axial Age—a fifth time of "starting over from
scratch."

"Children of chaos," Douglas Rushkoff has called us. "Without having physically migrated an inch, we have, nonetheless, traveled farther than any generation in history," he observes in *Playing
the Future*. Rushkoff is referring to things being not simply in con-
fusion and disarray but in a state of discontinuity. "The degree of
change experienced by the last three generations rivals that of a
species undergoing mutation," he notes.

six traits to think about

In *The New Religious Consciousness*, published in 1976, the sociologist Robert Bellah wrote, "I am reasonably sure that even though
we must speak from the midst of it, the modern situation represents
a stage of religious development in many ways profoundly different
from that of historic religion."

Thirty years later, it has become even more evident just how different things are in the religious realm today. At least six identifiable shifts in religious sensibility are worth noting as they relate to the future of the church.

The first is the issue of pluralism. Gordon Melton, an expert on new religious movements, writes:

> During the twentieth century, the West has experienced a phenomenon it has not encountered since the reign of Constantine: the growth of and significant visible presence of a variety of non-Christian and non-Orthodox Christian bodies competing for the religious allegiance of the public. This growth of so many religious alternatives is forcing the West into a new situation in which the (still) dominant Christian religion must share its centuries-old hegemony in a new pluralistic environment.

Chris Partridge, a theologian in Great Britain, says we are witnessing the "confluence of secularization and sacralization." This change, he says, is creating a new religiocultural milieu. Translation? Religion is evolving into an entirely new manifestation—one that may not have any connection to an institutional church.

It's interesting to me, for example, how many evangelical Protestant churchgoers also attend yoga, participate in silent retreats at Catholic monasteries, meditate daily, and sing the praises of Chinese acupuncture. While the theology in their head may keep them from explicitly exploring other religions, at a heart level they remain open to new spiritual practices.

Others, of course, have left the church entirely and now draw on alternative resources to meet all their spiritual needs. In an age of DVR and TiVo, a thirty-minute sermon programmed on a Sunday morning doesn't have the appeal it once had—not even as part of the total spiritual package. The new spiritual impulse manifests itself outside the confines of traditional religious notions about how faith is to be enacted (that is, by attending church). We're seeing the emergence of a nonreligious religiosity and a noninstitutional way of living out faith—the second shift in religious sensibility.

A two-hour television show called *Heaven*, hosted by Barbara Walters, explored various views regarding the concept of heaven. In her introduction to the show, Walters commented that "most of us don't get our information about heaven from religion" but instead get it from popular culture.

Eric Clapton's song "Tears in Heaven" and TV's animated *Simpsons* are as much a part of the churchgoer's consciousness today as passages from Revelation or any other biblical book—in fact, maybe more so. From early classics like *It's a Wonderful Life* to contemporary films like *What Dreams May Come,* "popular culture has become the receptacle for our collective imagination," said one of Walters's guests. In our current culture, it isn't the local church or pastor that is providing a compelling vision of the afterlife but musicians, filmmakers, and authors. Indeed, with the advent of the Internet, *anyone* can throw his or her ideas into the ring and get a hearing.

> In our current culture, it isn't the local church or pastor that is providing a compelling vision of the afterlife but musicians, filmmakers, and authors.

Once upon a time, the church controlled publishing. You couldn't get your religious book published unless it went through a battery of tests and was deemed to uphold orthodox theology. What's more, you often needed a sponsor to help pay for the project. If the sponsor didn't like your message, it died on the table—or still in your head (since you probably needed to pay a scribe or typesetter, too).

Today, the church just doesn't have that kind of control. It may still offer catechism classes, "discipleship" courses, and Christian maturity growth tracks in an effort to exert some control over the spiritual formation of congregants, but the reality is, any messages communicated in these settings must ultimately compete with thousands of others.

A third element worth noting is the impact of individualization. Jaspers made the following observation:

> If a transcendent aid does manifest itself, it can only be to free a man and by virtue of his autonomy, for he that feels free lets his beliefs fluctuate, regardless of any clearly defined credo . . . in accordance with an unfettered faith, which escapes any specific definition, which remains unattached while retaining the sense of the absolute and seriousness, along with their strong vitality.

Jaspers argued any new form of spirituality would have to address the issue of human freedom. Writing in the mid-twentieth century, he said, "This faith still has not found any resonance with the masses" and is "despised by the representatives of the official, dogmatic, and doctrinaire creeds." Fifty years later, however, the situation has changed. Alternative faith and spirituality have garnered more and more momentum, in spite of the church's best efforts to contain them.

Jaspers implied that the future of religion was to be found with the individual and not in church. Robert Bellah echoes this idea. "The symbolization of man's relation to the ultimate conditions of his existence is no longer the monopoly of any groups labeled religious. . . . Any obligation of doctrinal orthodoxy has been abandoned by the leading edge of modern culture."

He goes on to say that in the future, individuals will have to work out their own solutions to questions about the sacred. The "most the church can do is provide him a favorable environment for doing so, without imposing a prefabricated set of answers," Bellah writes.

A fourth issue that presents a great challenge to the institutional Christian church is the "this-worldliness" of the new spirituality. Barbara Walters's television show about heaven provided striking evidence of how disconnected most people who adhere to traditional religions are from this dynamic.

"Heaven is our home," said Ted Haggard, an evangelical pastor.

"The real life is the next life," said Imam Feisal Abdul Rauf from New York's al-Farah mosque.

"We are made for heaven," claimed Roman Catholic Cardinal McCarrick.

The new spirituality, by contrast, is much more focused on how we live in this world right now. Today, the prevailing belief is that how we live now affects what happens to us after death, whatever the future of human existence beyond the grave might be.

In *The History of Religions*, Joseph Kitagawa says that all the major traditional religions tend to have a negative view toward the physical life—something nearly all the guests on Walters's show seemed to confirm. An emphasis on life outside our current realm of existence, be it heaven or nirvana, inevitably produces the view that life in this world is less desirable, a sort of prison from which religion promises release.

> An emphasis on . . . heaven or nirvana implies that life in this world is less desirable, a sort of prison from which religion promises release.

Writing in the 1970s, Bellah said, "A radical change has taken place in the thinking of modern people, in that they no longer take seriously the existence of another realm of reality."

Though words like *heaven, paradise,* and *kingdom of God* are still used, Bellah noted that these terms now have purely symbolic meaning. "This phenomenal world is the only real order of existence, and life here and now is the center of the world of meaning," he observes. It isn't that no one believes in heaven and hell anymore, only that those ideas are no longer central to our culture's understanding of the nature and purpose of spirituality.

Obviously that's a problem for the church—indeed, for all the monotheistic faiths. For years, churches have declared that only those people who believe in their particular religion will get to heaven. It's what's communicated on Sunday, and it's what's said on national TV. When Walters asked representatives from each religion to describe heaven, they all expressed similar views. Without exception, each description seemed to paint a picture of the "good life"—a life that few experience here on earth. Mansions, servants, fine furnishings, good wine—these are the things we can look forward to in heaven. The message is clear: real life begins after death.

Kitagawa said that the challenge for modern religions is "to find the meaning of human destiny in *this* world—in culture, in society, and human personality." The vision of evolutionary spirituality is immanent and exists on earth as much as it does in heaven.

"I am much more interested in life before death than life after death," said the actor Richard Gere when Walters asked about his views on heaven. Meanwhile, the comedian and rabbi Jackie Mason said he hoped that heaven is just like earth.

The church has long divided the world into dichotomies such as sacred versus secular, saved versus lost, in versus out, and earthly versus heavenly. This is the fifth issue—the shift today toward a more holistic view rather than either-or dualism. The new spiritual impulse says that all the earth is sacred and that all of life is touched by God, not just the religious bits. Although some people might regard this change as a return to some sort of pagan superstition in which God is believed to reside in everything, including the trees and the rocks and the animals, it is not. The idea is that all

> The new spiritual impulse says that all the earth is sacred and that all of life is touched by god, not just the religious bits.

of life is a sacred whole. Evolving forms of the spiritual seek to create some kind of harmony with the world around us.

The sixth and final shift is that service, too, is no longer the exclusive domain of the church. Religion, at its best, has always been about service. Acts of compassion and charity have been the backbone of religious associations virtually since the inception of religion itself. But there is a rise in service by so-called secular groups, fueled, no doubt, by the increasing focus on global connectedness.

It's no longer just pastors or religious people calling society to care for its neighbors but rock stars and other celebrities. All the way back to George Harrison's Concert for Bangladesh in 1971 to Live Aid in the 1980s to the recent Live Eight concerts for Africa, pop culture—and pop musicians in particular—have championed a vision of philanthropic actions and ethics, entirely divorced from religious associations. Neither can we overlook TV programs such as *Extreme Makeover: Home Edition* where a team of people rally whole communities to aid one of their neighbors.

Anita Roddick, founder of the Body Shop stores, has a Web site and publishing company devoted to what she terms "spiritual activism." She spotlights various groups and people from around the world who are working to transform the world. Spiritual activists, religious change makers, and soulful rebels are all invited to share their stories to inspire and challenge others to play a part in the betterment of humanity.

On December 19, 2005, *Time* magazine announced an interesting trio of people as its Persons of the Year: "For being shrewd about doing good, for rewiring politics and reengineering justice, for making mercy smarter and hope strategic and then daring us to follow, Bill and Melinda Gates and Bono are *Time*'s Persons of the Year." Who is seen to be doing the most good in the world today— or at least having the most influence? Not the church, it seems, or any of its representatives, but the creator of Microsoft and his wife and a rock star.

Earlier, I mentioned that the world today is miles away from the one inhabited by Martin Luther. And yet it seems to me that to come to any conclusions about the future of the institutional church, we first need to understand its past.

money, money, money

In 1517, Johann Tetzel began working along the border of Saxony in northern Europe. As an emissary of the pope, Tetzel's job was to sell indulgences in congregations throughout medieval Europe.

Indulgences were big business for the church in the Middle Ages. Somewhat like the pledge drives of public television, the selling of indulgences provided financing for the ongoing work of the church. Indulgences kept the institution going. Of course, that's not how they were marketed. Tetzel's sales pitch included a happy little ditty, "As soon as the coin in the coffer rings, out from purgatory a soul springs."

The concept of indulgences was based on a doctrine that required sinners to not only repent of their sins but also confess them and pay some sort of earthly punishment, some form of penance. Though medieval Christians saw Christianity as an internal affair, they also believed there needed to be some outward demonstration of its influence in a person's life. They wanted to "see" the validity of a repentant sinner's claim.

So they developed the concept of "temporal punishments." Acts of charity, such as feeding the poor or caring for the sick, were required by all believers. They felt that a truly repentant person would naturally behave differently and more charitably to fellow human beings. But persons who died without fulfilling their temporary punishments would find themselves in purgatory, a sort of holding cell for souls after death.

This is where indulgences came in. Basically, they were "get out of jail free cards" for Christians who had committed sins. An indulgence might read, "By the authority of all the divine saints, and in every mercy toward you, I absolve you from all sins and misdeeds and remit all punishments for ten days."

Indulgences were sold to save people from the danger of purgatory—at least until they sinned again. Of course, because indulgences were temporary and not all-inclusive, sinners might need any number of them throughout the course of their lives.

And what was to be done about all the people who might have been in peril of purgatory when they died? As it turns out, the church was more than willing to let people buy indulgences to get deceased friends and family members out of their state of punishment, too.

The rise of indulgences was linked, of course, to the relatively new economic concept of mercantilism that was sweeping medieval Europe. Adopted from the Muslims around the twelfth century, mercantilism was the practice of transporting goods from one location to another and selling them for a higher price.

Mercantilism changed the way Europeans traded. Prior to this, trade was based on the barter system: "I'll trade you two chickens for my lamb." Mercantilism, by contrast, put money into circulation.

Amazing as it seems, trading with money in this manner was a relatively new concept, and it took a while for the Europeans to adjust. The reason money works is because it's made of a substance that has no value except what we ascribe to it (as opposed to coinage). When you walk into an Apple store to buy a brand-new video iPod, you hand the salesclerk a handful of paper with images printed on it, and the clerk hands you your product. The only reason this exchange takes place is because somewhere else, that paper can be traded for something useful and valuable. Money can be substituted for real things. In order for money to truly replace a barter economy, it had to have some value beyond its physical value.

Now, let's get back to the issue of indulgences. They were created by the church for one purpose only—to collect money. The medieval church was virtually the sole provider of welfare and social aid in the Middle Ages, and it needed money to pay for all that charity.

Initially, the church sent out proctors to beg for money. But it soon became apparent this wasn't the best way to become economically solvent. So in the thirteenth century, the church came up with the concept of indulgences. Applying the principles of mercantilism to the spiritual life, indulgences allowed people to pay someone, in this case the church, to do the good works demanded of them.

The church assumed that the clergy were probably doing more good works than required of them, so why not sell the extras? Even bishops could sell their indulgences with the approval of the pope, and they often did. The logic of indulgences was the same as the logic of money. In place of the real thing (good works), a worthless piece of paper was granted a value and used as a substitute.

Indulgences illustrate two important characteristics of the institutional church: first, its preoccupation with self-preservation, and second, the centuries-old tendency to shrink-wrap and sell grace.

Medieval Christianity operated with a sense of the fragile relationship between God and individuals. Why did indulgences work? Because people couldn't do enough good works and had a tendency to commit sins against God on a number of levels.

Sin, in the medieval church, was a complex issue. All kinds of sins had been isolated and labeled, based on their degree of severity. There were two major categories of sins: mortal and venial. Mortal sins were the worst kind—acts intentionally committed against God that, if not repented of, would result in the sinner's being condemned to hell. Venial sins were unintentional but still needed to be dealt with in order for the sinner to remain within God's grace.

Whatever the sin—and every imaginable kind was categorized in minute detail—a specific debt needed to be paid in order
for the sinner to "die in a state of grace" and gain access to heaven.
For those who might not make it all the way to heaven, there was
purgatory to face. Because of this dynamic, the sale of indulgences
flourished.

Although the practice of selling indulgences drew much criticism, it wasn't until an Augustinian monk named Martin Luther
noticed fewer of his congregants attending confession that anyone
seriously challenged the practice. Luther discovered that instead of
attending church, people were chasing after Tetzel and buying
indulgences.

Soon Luther began opposing the practice through his speaking and writing. His resistance to indulgences was based on his conviction that the Christian life was fundamentally a phenomenon of
the inner spiritual life of humans and had little to do with temporal
punishments in the outer world. Good works, penance, and especially indulgences had nothing to do with receiving God's grace.
Luther was convinced that those who follow God stood before him
by faith alone and nothing else.

Luther eventually took on the church when he placed his
Ninety-Five Theses—basically a tract against the selling of indulgences—on the church door in Wittenberg. For this and many
other subsequent actions, Luther was branded a heretic by the
church and excommunicated.

Luther's resistance to the sale of indulgences was a symptom
of a deeper feeling, expressed in what is possibly his most famous
concept, "justification by faith alone." For Luther, indulgences, lists
of doctrinal assents, and good deeds were irrelevant.

It's not that Luther thought the sacraments of the church
were unimportant. What Luther rejected was the church's method
of turning grace into a marketable commodity, something to be
bought and sold.

And yet in some ways, Luther's view of God was not so different from that of his peers. He was as much a product of his time as they were. He may have rejected the "selling of eternity" via indulgences, challenged the authority of the pope, and argued for new perspectives in the way the Christian church conducted itself, but he remained firmly committed to the medieval idea of how institutions should function. He desired to be a reformer, hoping to return the church to its earlier "innocent" state rather than looking forward to the future and the potential rebirth of the church.

What's ironic, of course, is that although Luther replaced the selling of indulgences, he went on to invent his own system of economics by which grace could be received. Built around his own views on the importance of the Ten Commandments, the Apostles' Creed, and the Sermon on the Mount, Luther's theory emphasized the internal concept of faith. Catholicism, on the other hand, focused on the issue of externals—good works as evidence of internal faith. Yet both were transactional business deals in one form or another.

INTERACT ONLINE
In fifty words or less, describe your
impression of the church today.

www.spencerburke.com/heretic/churchtoday

context and texture

Today, churches no longer offer paper indulgences, but the influence of mercantilism is still evident. As I see it, the church is still attempting to prop itself up by capitalizing on people's fear.

For as long as I've been a Christian, contemporary Christianity has been obsessed with not only sin but also the end of the world. Of course, today it seems apparent that perhaps it's not the end of history Christians fear so much as the end of the reason-based, linear view of history that has driven the Christian perspective.

For the past couple of hundred years, the church has been declaring the end of civilization as we know it and calling people to get on board in order to be saved from the coming apocalypse. The church's primary role seems to be making sure people believe the right things and accept the theology the church deems necessary for them. There is no wrestling, no questioning—just acceptance. "Accept Jesus into your heart, and you will go to heaven."

The only problem is that in twenty-first-century life, texture is just as important as content. How things look and feel and appeal to our senses is as important as any rational system of ideas to which we have no feeling of connectedness.

For many people, the experience of going to church is like going to a furniture store with an aggressive salesperson. You're interested in a couch, but the salesperson insists you have to buy a whole room full of furniture—end tables, lamps, bookcases, chairs, and even accessories. Making matters worse, there's no option for you to pick and choose items or even select colors or fabrics. You have to buy the whole package right now—because the sale is ending tomorrow.

In a chaotic world, texture is important. It is how we feel our way into the future. We desire to hold, feel, and struggle with ideas and issues of ultimate meaning. We don't need smoothly prepackaged concepts and constructs. We don't need people pressuring us to buy things we don't want just to get a commission or keep their store in business.

The Christian story as presented by the church is no longer resonating with the culture. People are not leaving churches because they've ended their spiritual journey or have abandoned their commitment to the teachings of Jesus. Nor are they trying to escape life or responsibility. This can't be written off as simply the effects of consumer culture. On the contrary, people are leaving the church because they want to embrace something more than abstract ideas and religious dogma. They want a transforming spirituality that gives their life shape and meaning. The *currency* of the church has to change.

> people are leaving the church because they want to embrace something more than abstract ideas and religious dogma.

Matthew Fox, the renegade former Catholic priest, put it this way:

> So much of religion in overdeveloped countries is on books, academic institutions, degrees, sermons, and words. While learning is essential to healthy religion, it is no substitute for praxis. Thinking about God is no substitute for tasting God, and talking about God is no substitute for giving people ways to experience God. Fewer and fewer people are attracted to Christianity in the "first world" countries because there is little practice, so little spirituality, in religion.

This is the dilemma of the church in the twenty-first century. As John Drane has said, "Christians have assumed Descartes was right, and have taken it for granted that the exercise of human reason is the way to understand things." He expands this idea a bit more by focusing on the fascination the church has with the modern age: "The reality is, however, that the church does, for the most part, seem to like the culture of modernity, and espouses its values as if they were in some absolute sense the truth."

Phyllis Tickle, the author of *God-Talk in America*, has noted, "In God-talk, as in every other form of earnest conversation, the environment in which the talking occurs is as central to the content of the discourse as is its grammar or its vocabulary or the logical flow of the argument."

The world is always part of our religious structures. There is no escaping it. I have no ax to grind with modernity. The issue is whether or not the church can connect meaningfully with the new world when it is so thoroughly entrenched in the old one.

Boundaries or Horizons?

The church, like most of the other traditional faiths in the last Axial Age, has opted for a boundary model. Boundary models are tribal by nature and function on the principle of exclusion. Explicit lines are drawn, allowing all to know whether they are in or out.

Inside the boundary, everything is prescribed and preordained. Every area of life has a specific set of answers at its heart, and any deviation from this course is branded as heresy. The focus of its instruction tends to be on the institution's survival.

I remember an "aha" moment in my own pastoral ministry when I realized that most of the sermons I heard—and indeed, most of the sermons I gave—were related to what the church should do, be, or look like. I spent hour after hour mining the letters of Paul to the various churches, scribbling down insights. Never mind that the New Testament didn't actually offer a very clear picture of the church—I was a man on a mission. And what about Jesus? To be honest, he usually only got a mention at the end of a service, when we used his name to invite people to join the church.

Boundary models are likely to be riddled with fear and suspicion toward those who live on the "outside." This is the model for "culture despisers," as the Old Testament scholar Walter Brueggemann called them. "The church is filled with people who value the faith, and for the sake of what they think is faith, they despise culture and all that means."

Not only does a model like this limit God's grace by placing it behind a wall of restrictions and requirements, but it also runs counter to Jesus' vision of a faith community that transcends religious and cultural limitations. Jesus' model was a kingdom, the "kingdom of God"—not a literal place limited by geography or border but a horizon, a new way of looking at the world around us. "Lift up your eyes and look on the fields," Jesus said. Change your perspective.

Some have attempted to live out Jesus' vision of a transcultural faith community. Thomas Merton, an American Trappist monk, took advantage of the revolutionary changes in the relationship between the Catholic church and non-Christian religions brought about by the Second Vatican Council in 1965 and became the first of his order to pursue contact with the East.

Merton wasn't merely interested in comparing notes with his Buddhist contemporaries. He wanted to be fully engaged. In an address he prepared for a convention in Calcutta, he wrote:

> I think that we have now reached a stage of (long overdue) religious maturity at which it may be possible for someone to remain perfectly faithful to a Christian and Western monastic commitment and yet learn in depth from, say, a Buddhist or Hindu discipline or experience. I believe some of us need to do this in order to improve the quality of our own monastic life and even to help in the task of monastic renewal which has been undertaken in the Western Church.

Unfortunately, Merton's life was cut short by a tragic accident, and the momentum of Vatican II was watered down over the years to the point where later popes reasserted the supremacy of Christian faith. But for a time at least, Merton blurred the lines and demonstrated that it is possible to adapt to changing cultural contexts and remain faithful to one's religious community. The Dalai Lama credits Merton with changing his views about Christianity. Another Buddhist, Thich Nhat Hanh, has written extensively about the relationship between his own faith and Christianity.

Merton was not alone in his endeavors. A number of significant Christian writers, thinkers, theologians, and leaders have attempted to rethink the possibility of a horizon-model version of Christian faith. To quote the writer Richard Holloway:

> One of the paradoxes of social and cultural change is that it is
> the people who are most determined to preserve institutions
> as they are who put them most at risk. . . . It is the morally
> adventurous, the people who question and challenge the status
> quo, who enable institutions to adapt to the future and maintain
> a developing life. It follows that the freedom to question is
> fundamental to moral and social revolution.

To some readers, the new spirituality may feel like the end of the world, but it's not. It's only the "end of the world as we know it," as Michael Stipe of R.E.M. sang. The world is not over. In fact, the future just got started. In this new situation, old systems must struggle to find their place again. Old rules no longer apply, and old institutions are no longer central to the purposes of society.

Is there a future for the Christian church as an institution? It's a difficult question to answer. Religions are remarkably resilient, and as some wise soul once said, "Old ages die slowly, if at all." But if the church is to survive, it will have to undergo some serious transformations. It will need to let go of interpreting the world in the old way and release the proprietary rights on Jesus.

The First Heretic?

Priscillian of Avila was the first person in the history of Christianity to be executed as a heretic. He was executed for the civil crime of performing magic, but it was his strong asceticism that got him into trouble.

As both an ascetic and a mystic, Priscillian believed that the Christian life was one of continual interaction with God. His favorite idea was expressed in the words of Saint Paul, "Know ye not that ye are the temple of God?" (1 Corinthians 3:16, KJV). To become a true temple for God, Priscillian argued that a person must renounce marriage and earthly honor and practice strict asceticism, hold to Catholic faith, and perform works of love.

It was on the issue of the renunciation of marriage that he got into trouble with the authorities. His eloquent arguments and severely ascetic lifestyle threatened the authority of the church. His opponents complained to Pope Damascus I, and a trial was held — in Priscillian's absence. Priscillian was found guilty of a number of offenses, mainly related to his extreme ascetic views and practices, and was beheaded in A.D. 385 under the orders of the Roman emperor Magnus Maximus.

Grace Held Hostage

> To think of Christ as the center and norm of
> all humanity made a certain sense in the
> Ptolemaic universe, which had the earth
> at its center. It continued to make some sense,
> however strained, in the Copernican universe,
> which had the sun at its center. Today,
> Christocentrism cannot make sense in the
> Einsteinian universe, which has **no center**
> and in which every structure is a dynamic
> relationality of **moving** components.
>
> —Tom F. Driver

I have been a part of the church in one form or another most of my life, including with a stint in a Christian commune, a stop at a well-known seminary, and twenty-two years as a "professional pastor." In 1998, I gave up being a pastor, and a few years later, I gave up membership in an institutional church altogether.

It's not that I'm angry at the church. It's just that I've become convinced that the future of faith doesn't lie exclusively there.

Some people insist that the church simply needs a make-over. In fact, saving religion seems to be what many people are attempting to do today by making it relevant, contemporary, and appealing to a largely disinterested public. They want to *reform* the church.

To be honest, I have no desire to reform the church. Unlike Luther, I'm for Protestant *transformation*, not reformation. Actually, my desire for change runs even deeper. I'm not just in favor of Protestant transformation. I'm for the transformation of all institutional faiths into something new and different.

I don't want to make Christianity hip or cool. A number of people are attempting to do this already. Will adding coffee and candles "fix" the church? Last time I checked, people weren't rejecting institutional religion because they didn't like the ambience; they're rejecting it because they don't relate to the message, the ideas, or the concepts it advances about God and life.

There's an interesting article titled "Marketing God" in an issue of *Gadfly*, a now-defunct pop culture magazine from Canada. A reporter had gone out to examine some churches that were attempting to appeal to younger people in the Minneapolis area. "There's no doubt that Generation X is largely unmoved by the language of traditional Christianity," observed the article's writer, Tyler Thoreson. "But I don't see many church leaders wondering if maybe the message itself is the problem."

Today, many churches think that because they use a DJ instead of a worship team, they are revolutionizing the message of Jesus. Let me be clear. I think it's great when a group decides to embrace a new form of technology and incorporate it into their worship experience. But if Jesus is basically presented in the same old way, using the same language, metaphors, and concepts, it really doesn't matter how much attention is paid to new technologies. The medium can't save the messenger.

When I was a pastor at Mariners Church in Irvine, Cali-

> if Jesus is basically presented in the same old way, . . . it really doesn't matter how much attention is paid to new technologies.

fornia, I actually had great flexibility in terms of style and approach. I worked with a terrific staff and had a wonderful caring team around me who were very open to new ideas. And yet one day it occurred to me that I really only had leeway to tinker with maybe 10 percent of what that particular institution was all about. The other 90 percent was off limits.

When I gave up pastoring, my family and I decided to attend Mariners' daughter church, Rock Harbor in Costa Mesa. I soon found myself as chair of the elder board, making critical decisions about the church's style, structure, and identity. Because we were a relatively new congregation and the average church attendee was only twenty-four years old, I found more flexibility to try new things—with maybe 20 percent of the institution up for discussion. We accomplished a lot and were extremely innovative in a number of areas. Still, every time it came to a vote, I found myself struggling. As innovative and creative as Rock Harbor was, as fresh and forward-thinking as its staff were, it was always going to be an event-driven institution. In time, I came to realize that to fight to make it anything else would mean hurting many people I cared for and respected. It might even destroy the church. Even though I had the authority to press these issues, I decided it would be better for me to make the transition. And so my quest for something beyond the church and institutional faith began.

To speak about moving beyond institutional faith is not an attempt at being cool as much as it is an acknowledgment that we live in a new age in which the restraints of religion inhibit the flow of God's grace into the world.

we live in a new age in which the restraints of religion inhibit the flow of god's grace into the world.

- I'm concerned when Jesus' death is brokered by Christianity simply as a business transaction.
- I'm concerned when institutional Christianity is so married to a particular political ideology that it supports policies and actions counter to the message of Jesus.
- I'm concerned when institutions demand their biblical interpretations to be the ultimate source of absolute truth and then use this truth to condemn and judge.
- I'm concerned when Christianity is presented as the only way to God.
- I'm concerned when institutions use the name of Jesus to maintain a patriarchal system that basically perpetuates women's status as second-class citizens.
- I'm concerned when the church says that a certain person or a particular group of people have no access to the grace of God because of their sexual orientation or because they grew up in some other part of the world under the influence of a different view of religion.

The root of Christian faith is Jesus' call to love passionately and radically. Yet that doesn't seem to be what the church is about these days.

propositional Religion

Instead, the church is known for dealing in propositions. It wasn't always this way, of course. In the Middle Ages, the focus was much more on faith as a "dynamic of the heart," not religion. As Peter Harrison has noted, "For the Church of the Middle Ages, the word 'faith' dominated theological discussion. 'Religion,' by way of contrast, had a restricted and technical use, referring to the 'state of life bound by monastic vows.' Thus to speak of the 'religions of England' in the fifteenth century was to refer to the various monastic orders."

Wilfred Cantwell Smith, in the classic book *The Meaning and End of Religion*, contended that it was only during the post-Reformation years, in the dawning Age of Reason, that the word *religion* came to mean a system of practices focused on the external aspects of religious life. "No one, as far as I have been able to ascertain, ever wrote a book specifically on 'religion' in the Middle Ages," he states.

Prior to the Reformation, there was only one church in the West, the Holy, Apostolic, and Catholic Church, which gave guidance and protection to all believers. *Catholic* meant simply "universal; including all people." But as Martin Luther challenged the direction of the church and tried to get it back to what he regarded as its true roots, the language changed. His efforts at reform ultimately caused the greatest division in the history of the Christian faith since the Great Schism of the eleventh century. Consequently, after the Reformation, religion came to mean a particular set of beliefs about faith that stood in opposition to the reformers' views. The reformers ushered in a new understanding of faith and perfected the art of propositional religion—a religion more about right beliefs than about simple faith. The Catholic version of Christianity was castigated as a "false religion," and Protestant beliefs were upheld as the "true religion." Thomas Cranmer's *Homily of Good Works*, published in 1547, speaks of "ungodly and counterfeit religions," which he determines are "papistical [Catholic] superstitions and abuses."

For centuries afterward, there were trials and persecutions of both Catholics and Protestants across Europe as each side attempted to position itself as the one true religion. As the theologian and author Graham Ward wrote, "'True religion' was embedded in a culture of violent hatreds; the Christian gospel of love was preached with the threats not of hell's fires only, but earthly fires also and instruments of torture."

Around this same time, the idea of "world religions" also came into existence. We talk about world religions as though they have always existed. Of course, many have, but again, not in the way we understand them today. The conversation about other faiths is itself a product of the Reformation. To quote Peter Harrison again:

> The "world religions" were thus generated largely through the projection of Christian disunity onto the world. It follows that much of the perceived conflict between the so-called world religions can be attributed to the grammar of the term "religions." . . . It would be foolish to deny, of course, that a belief in reincarnation is radically different to a belief in resurrection of the body, or of immortality of the soul. But we must question whether such differences are as significant as the concept of "a religion," propositionally conceived, makes them out to be.

It's interesting that the concept of multiple religions didn't find its way into the English vocabulary until almost the end of the sixteenth century and even then didn't become commonly used for another few decades.

In *Nothing Sacred*, Douglas Rushkoff wrote about his own faith: "The faith of Israel, then—what we call Judaism—was born not out of the acceptance of a belief, but out of a willingness to challenge one's beliefs." He went on to bemoan the actions of a Jewish leader at a synagogue he visited who was

> turning Judaism into a set of sacred and inviolable truths. He was sacrificing our iconoclasm, our abstract monotheism, and our community-driven ethos to an oversimplified set of pat answers that were to be accepted on faith. Intelligent inquiry, textual literacy, and genuine engagement were to be surrendered. And this rabbi truly believed he was doing a good thing. He thought he was saving a religion.

The institutional church has come to be known over the years for its obsession with boundaries. It seems to spend so much of its time monitoring other people to see what they are and aren't doing. It creates formulas to determine who's in and who's out, who's lost and who's saved. On the occasions when these formulas don't seem to work, the church often tries to strong-arm the situations and explain them away with phrases like "lack of faith" or "blinded by the devil."

The Christianity most of us are familiar with is built on answers. I was raised on a "Jesus is the answer" form of the faith, which implied that Christianity is the definitive answer to every single one of life's problems—even those that are not specifically addressed in the Bible. Imagine my surprise, then, to hear Alan Jones of Grace Cathedral in San Francisco say that the "task of the Christian minister is to guard the great questions."

Indeed, that's the very thing institutional churches today generally don't do. They don't ask questions. They present answers— answers to questions that people in our culture aren't even asking. Institutional faith is struggling today because it is formulaic and knowledge-based in a world that is fluid, flexible, and open to new ways of learning and interacting.

> institutional faith is struggling today because it is formulaic and knowledge-based in a world that is fluid, flexible, and open to new ways of learning and interacting.

The separation of church and Hate

The institutional church is also struggling because of its tendency toward hate. I have a collection of photos and images on my laptop, and two images stand out to me. The first is of a man in a cowboy hat standing outside a nondescript building in Montana holding a large white placard that reads, "God Hates Fags." The second photo comes from Belfast and also features a gathering of people holding signs. The main sign is bright yellow and has a single word inscribed in black—"SIN." The people holding that sign are surrounded by others carrying smaller signs that read, "Sodomy is a sin."

Both photos represent something of the public face of Christianity. Both groups are protesting homosexuality. The Montana photo was taken outside the funeral of Matthew Shepard, the young man beaten and left hanging on a fence to die in the snow because of his sexual orientation. The Belfast shot was taken outside the city hall where government-sanctioned civil ceremonies for gay couples were being held.

Time and again, institutions seem to use their religious views as a pretext for an aggressive and adversarial posture against the wider culture. The issue of gay rights is just one of the many issues where this tendency emerges. The beauty of the message of Jesus so often gets lost in a destructive symbolism that rants and snarls at the world but seldom inspires longing for newness or a finer way of being human.

Another recent example of this negative symbolism has been the issue of Supreme Court nominees and the high-profile lobbying of certain Christian groups. Churches linked up by satellite to a gathering of religious and political leaders, demanding that the nominees fit their criteria. And sadly, I heard the televangelist Pat Robertson characterize Israeli Prime Minister Ariel Sharon's stroke as "God's retribution for giving away Israel."

It's remarkable how often the visible representation of the church in culture is negative. There seems to be so much anger and hatred in the name of Christianity. The popular cultural stereotype of Christians as a bunch of uptight, angry, joyless, and dogmatic people is usually affirmed at least once a week by some knee-jerk comment or action—someone predicting God's judgment on a city for banning the theory of intelligent design in schools, for instance, or calling down hell and brimstone on towns that refuse to have a manger scene on public lands during the year-end holidays. Contrary to popular belief, anger—even so-called "righteous" anger—will never change the world. It takes a different kind of power to do that.

Noah Levine, a former punk who discovered spirituality and wrote a book about it called *Dharma Punx*, said recently, "Anger makes us stiff, and it is difficult to act out of anger; compassion makes you much more able and active to effect change in the world." Only the power of radical love and grace can accomplish the change we seek.

The message of Jesus is about making connections with each other and rooting the world in the love of God. Perhaps that sounds a little too idealistic given the realities of the world around us. But believing we can struggle together to love and serve each other in mutual respect and compassion is not out of touch with reality. It is to be in touch with the ultimate reality. It is to be in touch with God.

> The message of Jesus is about making connections with each other and rooting the world in the love of god.

Love your enemies. Do good to those who hate you. Bless those who curse you. Pray for those who abuse you. Treat others as you would have them treat you. These are the kinds of things Jesus said to do, and you don't have to become religious or believe a set of prescribed things about him in order to do them. Carter Heyward, theology professor and priest, has noted, "Jesus' teachings reflect an assumption that unless we are allowing the spirit of love, mutuality, and justice to work through us, nothing we do or say will affect evil, other than strengthen it." These are wise words for times when so many people are resorting to verbal or physical violence to assert themselves.

A fundamental shift

One of the surprising dynamics of the twenty-first century is the global emergence of fundamentalism in institutional faiths. Fundamentalism used to be the exclusive domain of Christians. Originating in the early twentieth century when a scientific view of the world threatened to replace a religious one, fundamentalism was concerned with stemming the tide and maintaining a certain understanding of the Bible.

This brand of fundamentalism provided the inspiration for that great old black-and-white film *Inherit the Wind,* starring Spencer Tracy. The movie documented the Scopes "monkey trial" of the 1920s, which depicted the struggle between a biblical explanation and an evolutionary explanation for human origins and was itself instrumental in the emergence of the fundamentalist movement.

Fundamentalism today—even Christian fundamentalism— is much more about the issues and challenges posed to religion by the global situations. Today's fundamentalists want to get back to something other than what we have now, which is perceived as a threat to a way of life and a set of values long held by institutional religions.

As Graham Ward rightly noted, there have always been communities of faith that declared themselves the upholders of true forms of the faith, but today's fundamentalists are publicly assertive in ways that previous groups were not.

The Iranian novelist Salman Rushdie, who lived for many years under the threat of death for committing "crimes against Islam" in his writing, said recently in an interview that "fundamentalists believe that we believe in nothing. We must prove them wrong by knowing what matters."

"Mythinformation"

All brands of fundamentalism seem to mix power-based interpretations of foundational documents with nostalgic views of the past. But nostalgia is not the answer to the present. What we need is imagination.

Institutional Christians tend to have a very narrow and literal interpretation of the Bible. Christianity is the only way to reach God, certain Christians argue, because the Bible says so. It tell us that Jesus said, "I am the way and the truth and the life. No one comes to the Father except through me." Yet as the theologian Maggi Dawn has said, "We cannot simply say 'the Bible says'; we need to account for our interpretation, and its application to the life of the Church in its present setting."

So how do I interpret this particular Scripture? In the next chapter, I'll explore it more fully, but I don't believe it can be used to argue that Christianity is the only true religion. First, Christianity as a religion didn't exist when Jesus spoke these words. Compounding this point are two additional facts: no one actually recorded Jesus' words at the time he spoke them, so we have no proof that they are indeed his words, and what he did say, he said in Aramaic, which means that nothing in the Bible as translated into any other language can be taken literally anyway. Moreover, Jesus lived and died a Jew, so whatever he said must be read in light of that. Second, Jesus' concept of the world was vastly different from mine. But more important, to read this as a literal statement requires that I take the other statements he makes about himself as literal. For example, Jesus declares that he is the bread and the vine and the Good Shepherd. Does that mean he is literally a loaf of bread or a plant? Of course not! These are metaphors, clues to something about his character and person.

Of course, most preachers today compound the problem by trying to apply the Scripture to people outside the church as well as

those inside, which is why this Scripture gets used a lot to assert
Christian superiority in the global religious economy. About this
tendency, Maggi Dawn said that in order "for Christian hermeneutics [interpretation of texts] to remain truly Christian, we must avoid
treating [Scripture] as a means of preserving a historical religion in
terminal decline, and instead expect it to voice the living truth of
Christ."

In our commitment to the Bible, we have to account for the
ways in which we interpret Scripture. We cannot just approach it
like a rule book, guide book, maintenance manual, database, or any
of the other analogies I have heard used over the years to describe
what the Bible is. We cannot pull isolated verses of Scripture out of
context to make a case for our own particular prejudices and
biases—though we all have done it, myself included!

"Every generation, on the basis of its own social and cultural
history, tradition, education, and experiences, reads the Bible in
ways that our ancestors would not recognize. This is because we
always read the texts of our own lives in relation to the biblical text,"
Carter Heyward observes.

It might just be, as Douglas Rushkoff has argued, that the rise
of fundamentalist rhetoric and action is a symptom of our inability
to reinterpret and recontextualize the metaphors of our faith in such
a way that they mean something new and fresh to us again. "The ex-
ploitation of metaphor for the installation of fearful obeisance demands a horrible ending," he writes. "We are not allowed to grow
up. . . . If we cling to the metaphors we were given as children, we
will surely perish. They no longer adequately describe our personal
or global experience."

It is not that the Bible doesn't have anything to say to the
world today or that Jesus means nothing in the new global economy.
It is more likely that we put the wrong words into his mouth. Somewhere along the way, we have assumed that to be faithful to the tradition, we must simply reiterate what has been said before, in

exactly the same way. But this is not faithfulness, nor does it keep us in step with tradition.

Real tradition is not an institutionalized form of faith or the artifact of a past that is never to return. It is alive—a force that anticipates and informs the present. We ask questions of the Bible that our ancestors would not have conceived, questions about nuclear technology, global capitalism, genetic engineering, and a host of others issues that make life challenging. As we approach Scripture with these questions, the Bible changes. It changes because we read into and from it new issues, new questions, and new challenges. It grows, and so do we. We approach it as a living text, believing that it can speak to our lives today even though it was written long ago, and then we attempt to set its meaning in stone. But you can't have it both ways.

It is also worth remembering that the Bible is not the source of Christian faith; Jesus is. The living word, not the written one, is our foundation. This doesn't mean I don't believe in the Bible—it informs my faith in Jesus. As a friend recently said, we have to embrace the Bible as the wild, uncensored, passionate account of

> it is worth remembering that the Bible is not the source of christian faith; Jesus is.

people experiencing the living God and not view it simply as a legalistic and static document.

Rejecting capitalist Religions

Another primary charge people level against institutional faiths, and Christianity in particular, is that it is preoccupied with money. In one sense, it's true. Were it not for religious institutions, there would be little in the way of welfare and help for many people in the world. Religion has been central in aiding the underprivileged and dispossessed throughout history—and it needs money to do so.

But it is also true that religion often turns its ideas about the sacred into business models that create a producer-consumer relationship between individuals and institutions. "You can't get something for nothing," religion says. Grace says otherwise.

> "You can't get something for nothing," religion says. grace says otherwise.

The business model of institutional Christianity is still largely medieval and based on some kind of exchange. It may not be good works. It might be faith. But in either case, it is understood to be based on a "give to get" mentality, and more and more people are resistant to this kind of deal-making between God and humanity. As the author and Christian ethics professor Beverly W. Harrison has said, we have had enough of "capitalist spirituality." I would be tempted to say we have had enough of capitalist *religion*, rather than capitalist *spirituality*, but the point is basically the same. Any form of religion that trades in commodities about God is increasingly being rejected in favor of a new working model.

In the Middle Ages, religion was affected by changes in trade and leadership models, which were related to new understandings of state relations. The flourishing idea of Christendom paralleled a new stability in Western society, expansions in trade, and developments in technology.

The idea of Christendom gained momentum somewhere in the ninth century and shaped the focus and future of the institutional form of Christian religion for centuries.

Christian faith and Christendom are not the same thing, although many people both inside and outside the church assume that they are. What makes Christendom different from Christianity is a particular attitude toward the idea of conversion. In Christendom, one is converted into the culture of the Christian religion. In Christian faith, conversion is to something else entirely, as we'll see later.

The concept of Christendom is even now only slowly giving way to something else among a large swath of the Christian church. Christian faith expressed outside of this construct seems almost inconceivable to some. Peter Brown, in *The Rise of Western Christendom*, notes that "Christendom was a notion that now carried the charge of perpetuity." No wonder we can't let go.

There was a sense in which medieval Christianity wanted to govern the earth, much like any other kingdom or state in the world. In fact, that is exactly how it viewed and interpreted its role: as ambassador for the kingdom of God. The church's view was that Jerusalem, the Holy City, was at the center of the Christian world ruled by the church. Similarly, Rome was viewed as the center of the medieval world, with the holy church at its very heart.

The pope waged wars and engaged in politicking and statecraft much like other rulers. The Crusades were a battle, not just between competing ideologies but between competing kingdoms — the kingdom of heaven represented by the church and the kingdom of the world represented by all those outside the authority and rule of the Holy See. The goal was to bring everybody into the church and do away with the non-Christian options. Everybody was to become Christian. It was the cultural religion of the Western world, and it aspired to be the religion of the entire world. Christianity *was* the culture, if you like.

Alan Kreider has offered some defining characteristics of key aspects of Christendom, which are helpful in thinking about the future of Christian faith. They help show us how a particular view of religion and religion's purpose in society emerged and why it is no longer a helpful model. I have adapted his ideas as they relate to this book.

Christendom is an attempt to bring all human experiences under the reign of Jesus Christ, whose role in society is mediated and shaped by the church. While there are differences between Luther's view of Christendom and other views that exist today, there are also a number of similarities worth noting that are related to ways we believe, belong, and behave.

- The belief system of Christendom is rooted in orthodox Christianity as affirmed by the church. This system is what gives shape to the society. It is the structural ideology touching all aspects of human life and experience. Whether people practice it or not, these beliefs provide the social and religious context for all peoples.

- In Christendom, right belief is essential, and heresy is not tolerated. No rival beliefs are permitted, as unity and truth are supremely important. The church banned heresy before it attempted to ban other religions. Christendom is like a one-party state, with no opposition parties allowed. Ideas can be debated, but one can never depart from the creedal documents.

- In Christendom, religious instruction is often basic. In fact, it is often assumed that people who live in a Christian society should know what its beliefs and practices are.

- In Christendom, the society's art and symbols are Christian. It goes without saying that Christian themes pervade a Christian society. Even today, the vapor trail of Christianity has left its mark on contemporary culture. This is why we can easily identify "Christ figures" in movies like *The Matrix*.

- In Christendom, everyone is a Christian and an inhabitant of a parish. People are Christians not because they necessarily believe but because they belong, and their belonging is rooted in geography as well as national identity. Outsiders are not generally tolerated—hence the expulsion of peoples such as the Jews from Europe during the Middle Ages.

- The relationship between church and state is mutually reinforcing. Whereas the United States has a separation between church and state, much of Europe has a state church. The relationship in both cases is symbiotic. Each institution affirms and supports the other. The church is society's symbolic center.

- In Christendom, there is a lack of choice. One must belong to the orthodox church or suffer the consequences. Punishments and laws require church attendance and giving.

- In Christendom, the basic division is not between the church and the world but between the clergy and the laity. A professional clergy with its own hierarchy is separated from ordinary Christians by things like ordination. The clergy serves the populace by offering religious guidance.

- In Christendom, behaving like a Christian is linked with "plain common sense." Christian behavior is virtually indistinguishable from the rest of society. This behavior is enforced by a number of layers of external influence from clergy all the way to legislated morality.

The schism between Catholics and Protestants split Christendom into two competing camps, but they both saw as their task the assertion of Christendom as a geographical location as well as a spiritual idea. In both camps, the view was that the church was to govern the earth in the name of Jesus and under the authority of God.

We no longer live within the confines of medieval Christendom. It is debatable if we ever did, but the shadow of the idea still remains. In Christendom, the pressure to be a Christian was pretty intense. Life could get messy if one resisted, and the history of Western civilization seems to highlight just how tough it could be. Even a brief reading of Christian history seems to show just how many people turned to Christian faith as a matter of convenience as much as conviction.

But these days, we live under a different economy. There are many within the Christian church who still wish to pressure people to convert to their particular view of things. But like it or not, the shifts we have experienced over the past century or so have made

> Religion cannot be advanced by compulsion, and wherever that tactic is attempted, it is usually rejected by all but the weakest of souls.

these attempts far less successful than they might otherwise have been. Religion cannot be advanced by compulsion, and wherever that tactic is attempted, it is usually rejected by all but the weakest of souls. "Coercion is not God's way of working," said one wise sage of the early church.

More and more people are turning away from the church and looking for other options. The economics of grace and the economics of religion have little in common. This is why I contend that grace is bigger than religion. Grace is a concept too wild to be held by any one entity, particularly when that entity is locked into a view of its function and role that is no longer beneficial to most people.

New Economies of soul

The move toward spirituality in today's world can be linked to new concepts about the way we engage with each other. Business models have shifted dramatically, but churches still tend to function on old models, driven by the concept of Christendom.

My former employer, Mariners Church, draws congregants from four counties and a radius of one hundred miles. If this is a parish church, then the boundaries of what makes it so must be radically redrawn. The members of the congregation drive past literally scores of other churches to make their way to this particular one. They seem to feel no obligation to go to their local evangelical church, or any other church closer to them, for that matter. It is choice, not compulsion, that motivates religious affiliation today.

Surprisingly, however, the present-day church often still looks and functions much like it did in the Middle Ages. The church still wishes to be the final authority in matters related to faith and belief. It still wants everyone to convert to its particular understanding of salvation and the divine. It still wants to make belief ordinary by compacting it into a simple matter of accepting predigested concepts.

Around the world, institutions of all kinds are accepting the challenge to change in order to survive, but the church seems stagnant, locked into a particular relationship with society. Christian bookstores are filled with books on leadership models for churches, most of them paralleling what is happening in the business world. But the concept of what the church is seldom gets addressed or changed. For instance, more and more companies are developing new leadership structures that focus on interdependence and move away from hierarchical structures, but churches still tend to be locked into the latter.

"Hierarchy is an organization with its face toward the CEO and its ass toward the customer," General Electric's CEO Jack Welch reportedly said. I couldn't agree more. Hierarchies exist to please the man (or woman) at the top, not the customer at the bottom. That can't be the best model for a fast-paced culture where the consumer is king.

Hierarchy is an interesting word. It was introduced by a Greek named Dionysius the Aeropagite more than fifteen hundred years ago in his treatises known as *Celestial Hierarchy*. For him, it referred to the "orderly arrangement of all sacred things taken together." The goal of such a perspective was to connect people with God and to create "the continued love of God and divine things, a life divinely sanctified into oneness with him."

When we think about hierarchy today, we think of bureaucracy and rigid pyramid structures seeking to monopolize information and power. According to the Swedish economists Kjell Nordstrom and Jonas Ridderstrale, this way of organizing humans into a "holy and harmonious order," as Dionysius put it, quickly came to mean ruling thorough the sacred. This organizational system builds on three key assumptions: a stable environment, predictable processes, and known output. In other words, you know where you are, what you do, and what will happen.

It's easy to see why such a model doesn't work today. Very little is stable in today's world. Everything is in a state of flux, and outcomes are subject to any number of unpredictables. What we do with our lives changes by the moment.

gold watch thinking

The father of a friend of mine worked for the same company for forty-three years. When he retired, he received a gold watch for all of his sacrifice and commitment. There aren't many gold watches handed out anymore because people have changed their working habits. Lifelong employment and the security it offered used to be an aspiration for many people. Our occupations defined us and gave us a sense of identity. "What do you do?" has long been an icebreaker when meeting people for the first time.

Gold watches symbolize a different time and place from the world I inhabit today. We have a different work ethic today. My friend's father's life was interwoven with the machinery of the company he worked for. He was a cog in its chain, company property from nine to five, five days a week. He thought nothing of this; it was just the ways things were. You did your work; you got your pay; after forty-three years, you got your gold watch. That's how the world worked.

My work world is entirely different. I seldom put in a forty-hour week, and I don't go to a factory or an office. Like many people today, I work from home. Well, actually, I work in the garage or sometimes in front of the television. I fly to conferences around the world. My work is feast or famine. I do a number of different things, most of them built around choices and decisions I have made about quality of life and things I want to experience.

My friend's father's working life was more influenced by Luther than mine is. One of Luther's well-known sayings was related to how we think about work: *ore et labore*—pray and work. In Luther's view, work was a good thing in and of itself and was best viewed as an act of worship and self-improvement, whatever the work might be. Luther's view on labor is one of the roots of the capitalist society. We work hard, and life gets better. This view of life as work and work as life no longer holds the imagination of people as it once did. More and more people are trying new careers, following their muse, and viewing work as a means to an end, not the end itself. Work is necessary, but it is not the sum of who we are. Rather than gold watches, we want golden experiences.

Just as the old hierarchal business structure no longer satisfies workers who are looking for more meaning in life, organized religion fails to provide the golden spiritual experiences we seek. When people say they don't like organized religion, they usually mean they don't like institutions. There is a difference between organization and institutionalization, but we seldom nuance our prejudice. What we reject is the controlling style of modern institutions. We no longer trust that institutions have our best interests at heart. And this alienation that most people feel toward highly organized and bureaucratic structures is barely felt by those inside the system.

The Christian church is a hodgepodge of different versions of institutional models, and this is why many people reject it. The Catholics still practice a kind of high-medieval model with the pope as the supreme leader of a global multinational. Protestant churches like the Anglican have a similar model. It is less authoritarian but has a similar leadership structure. Most contemporary churches have a more modern bureaucratic version of the institution, with the pastor functioning as the CEO. Whatever their particular model, most churches are still versions of hierarchical structures, and this is no longer viable in today's society. This structure is too sluggish. It cannot move with changing times. Of course, institutions don't really want to change with the times. They would rather remain the same and control the market.

I said earlier that hierarchy means to rule through the sacred. But, in truth, the sacred is not meant to be subject to anyone's rule. And yet the Christian church wants not only to rule *through* the sacred but also to rule *over* the sacred. Like all institutions, it desires to control and dominate the market. It wants be the sole proprietor of God's grace, acting as the doorkeeper, if you will. No corporation exists to simply get by. The goal is always to profit, expand, and dominate the market.

The business of religion is the sacred in all its forms. Christianity's part of that business is grace. The church wants to put a copyright on grace and seeks to hold power and control over it by making itself the only mediator. "Grace is available only through us, and you must come to us to gain access to it," declares the church. Determining who is in and who is out is the primary way that the church as institution tries to control grace.

Jesus told a story about this in the gospel of Matthew. It concerned a wheat farmer who had spent a hard day planting. While he was sleeping, his enemy crept onto his land and sowed weeds among the wheat. When the wheat began to sprout, the laborers noticed the weeds growing, so they went to the landowner and asked him if they should pull up the weeds. "'No,' he answered, 'because while you are pulling up the weeds, you may root up the wheat with them. Let both grow together until the harvest. At that time I will tell the harvesters: First collect the weeds and tie them in bundles to be burned; then gather the wheat and bring it into my barn.'"

This story reflects the tendency humans have to want to do God's business. Institutional religion usually aspires to do the landowner's job—God's job. They want to determine who is wheat and who is weed.

Churches assume their role is about eternity when in fact eternity is God's business. The landowner in Jesus' story is very clear that his workers cannot separate the wheat from the weeds, for they might pull up perfectly good wheat in their zeal to remove the wayward weeds. When explaining this story to his followers, Jesus makes it clear that the task of determining who is in or out is not the responsibility of humans, no matter how qualified they believe they are. I would likewise argue that the church should not be so focused on eternity. The church's task is to help people follow Jesus here on earth.

INTERACT ONLINE

In your opinion, what will the institutional church need to let go of in order to move into the future?

www.spencerburke.com/heretic/thefuture

The survival instinct

Like most institutions, the church has a desire to survive. To do that, it must follow certain laws. One of the primary laws of institutional survival is that the majority takes precedence over the minority. Institutions have to place more value on their own survival than on individual survival. As the late advertising guru Tibor Kalman once said, "Religion works better for corporations than for people."

There are examples of this corporate institutional dynamic at work in the New Testament and involving Jesus himself. In John's gospel, the Jewish religious leaders—Pharisees and other groups—got together to discuss what they should do about Jesus, who was increasingly becoming a threat to the status quo.

"What are we accomplishing?" they asked. "Here is this man
performing many miraculous signs. If we let him go on like this,
everyone will believe in him, and then the Romans will come
and take away both our place and our nation." Then one of
them, named Caiaphas, who was high priest that year, spoke up,
"You know nothing at all! You do not realize that it is better for
you that one man die for the people than that the whole nation
perish."

Jesus' death was expedient for the Jews, in Caiaphas's opinion. The
institution, or in this case the nation, must take precedence.
Caiaphas, John's gospel goes on to say, had "prophesied" that Jesus
had to die. He made this declaration because the survival of the Jews
rested on it happening according to the logic of his religious ideology.

This logic of religious survival is often at odds with the message and life of Jesus. Jesus was supremely interested in the individual life and went to great lengths to honor and support every person
he met. His whole life stands as a metaphor of what can happen
when the individual is sacrificed for the greater good, and the stories he told are filled with this idea. For instance, Jesus said that a
good shepherd would leave his ninety-nine sheep in the wilderness
to go look for one lost sheep—hardly a smart move if you wish to
keep the rest of your flock safe. When he was asked how many times
we should forgive a person who has embezzled us again and again,
Jesus replied, "Seventy times seven."

Four hundred and ninety times we should forgive the same
person for the same offense. To put it another way, there is no limit
to forgiveness, even for those who are glaringly guilty.

In perhaps his most startling challenge to the tendency of religious hierarchies to sacrifice the individual for sake of the institution,
Jesus defended his disciples' violation of Sabbath law by saying that
their hunger superseded laws made in God's name. In Mark's story,
he says, "The Sabbath was made for man, not man for the Sabbath."

These responses from Jesus run counter to the pragmatic and expedient way institutions function. Focusing attention on the individual runs counter to the corporate mentality. Plato said that a ship could be steered to reach its destination only by a single captain and an obedient crew. This is how the ship of faith has been running for centuries, which is probably why Jesus never actually told anyone to start a religion in his name.

how we lost the plot

The twentieth century was meant to be the "Christian century," according to its nineteenth-century proponents. Many Christians were so convinced of this eventuality that they adopted slogans like "the evangelization of the world in this generation." This was the clarion cry of the First International Convention of the Student Volunteer Movement in 1891—the largest-ever gathering of students up to that time. Given the expanse of the British Empire and the growing machinery of the American brand of capitalist expansion, there was probably some support for this kind of triumphant thinking. The reality turned out to be somewhat different.

Rather than triumphing, the nineteenth century's leading faith was greatly weakened by all that happened over the course of the twentieth century. It wasn't just the incredible loss of life incurred through wars, dictatorships, and genocides; it was also the perception that Christianity had nothing to say to any of these things. When it did speak, its answers to things like the existence of evil and violence rang hollow—much as they do today.

But this is not a bad thing. In some ways, this bodes well for Christian faith. No longer living with the myth of Christendom or Christian dominance means that the temptation to aspire to power has been greatly reduced. It has also cleared the stage of old stories and made room for new ones to be told.

Interestingly enough, Jesus remains a figure of interest to many people today, in spite of the church's loss of favor and influence and despite the incredible changes in our world. "Jesus is just all right with me," sang the Doobie Brothers in the early 1970s. He is still all right with a lot of people today. *"Les religions passent, mais Dieu demeure,"* as Victor Hugo put it—"Religions pass away, but God remains." It is almost as if Jesus has freed himself from the constraints of religion, and we are now free to explore grace beyond restraint.

The Irish singer and activist Sinead O'Connor summed it up this way: "Rescuing God from religion is how I'd put it. All these rules and regulations and locked doors keep God a prisoner who cannot be shared unless we do this, or do that, or the other."

6

Faith Remixed: The Fine Art of Bricolage

For a thousand years, Christianity penetrated deeply into the lives of people, enduring Reformation, Enlightenment and industrial revolution by adapting to each new social and cultural context that arose. Then, really quite suddenly in 1963, something very profound ruptured the character of the nation and its people, sending organised Christianity on a downward spiral to the margins of social significance. . . . The cycle of inter-generational renewal of Christian affiliation, a cycle which had for many centuries tied the people however closely or loosely to the churches and to Christian moral benchmarks, was permanently disrupted by the "swinging sixties."

—Callum Brown

Every month or so, Lisa, the kids, and I meet up with friends at the park for a picnic—except we don't call it a picnic. We call it church.

When we get there, my eight-year-old son, Alden, crawls around under the bushes inviting people to join us. "Hey, we've got some buckets of chicken and salads over there. You want to come join us?"

I'm always amazed at how many people take us up on the offer, and for that matter, just how many people actually live in the park. We always bring enough food for fifty people and sometimes some extra goodies.

One week, my daughter, Gracie, discovered she'd outgrown some of her shoes. "We should take them to the park," she suggested, recalling the little girls she'd seen the last time we were there. "Yeah, and I've got some old Halloween costumes," Alden piped up. "Halloween is coming up. Maybe some of the kids would like to have them."

So that's what we did. We took Gracie's shoes, Alden's old Halloween costumes, and more buckets of chicken and salad. Gracie also brought some Barbie dolls to give away that week. When one of the ladies spied the dolls' golden hair sticking out of the bag, she could hardly contain her excitement. "Is that a wig?" she asked. She had cancer, and her hair had fallen out.

"No, it's a Barbie," explained Gracie.

Another woman said, "Oh, we have a number of little girls back at the hotel. Can I bring these back to them?"

Gracie said, "Sure, and this one's for you."

The woman's heart melted. Turns out she'd never had a Barbie as a child. Her eyes teared up, and she gave Gracie a big hug. She said, "I've always wanted one. Thank you. Thank you."

Meanwhile, Alden quickly rummaged through the bag. "I've got something for you," he said to the woman with cancer, proudly pulling out part of his old clown costume. "Look—it's a wig!" The woman laughed. In an instant, she went from having no hair to having huge rainbow-colored hair, but you know what? She was thrilled to get it. It was such a beautiful moment—a moment that, to me, captures the essence of church—not the institutional church, but church in its most innocent form. Alden and Gracie saw the need, and they wanted to meet it.

Now don't get me wrong. I'm not saying that a bucket of chicken is the solution to the institutional church's problems. Nor am I saying that everything would be fixed if we just did away with buildings, sat on blankets under the trees, and wore clown wigs. What I am saying is that there's something good about doing here and now the things that Jesus did back then. There's something good about *being* the church, not just going to church. And there's something good about faith, unshackled and unplugged.

The Beginning, or Maybe the Middle, but Not the End

Ever turn on religious television? Most of Christian TV is filled with people excited at the prospect of Jesus' return and the end of the world. How can a religion be so turned around that its adherents would wish, even *pray*, for the end of the world? And yet this seems to be some religions' focus today—driving the world ever closer to some kind of apocalypse, be it Christian, Muslim, or some other version. In their zeal, sad to say, I think most TV preachers—and even most pastors—have spent so much time talking about how Revelation demonstrates the end of the world that they've missed what is really being revealed.

A revelation shows us what we're not seeing. It is more about awakening than about destruction. It is illusion-shattering, like blinders falling from your eyes, allowing you to see something so clearly that you cannot imagine how you didn't see it that way before. Institutional Christianity tends to see life through a lens that has been conditioned to focus only on what is negative and what is wrong. Escape from the world is the only logical interpretation of redemption from this point of view, coupled with an almost ab-solute contempt for anything not officially sanctified as serviceable for the kingdom.

But as I see it, John's poetic, enigmatic, and sometimes dis-turbing vision is not so much a revelation about the end of the world as it is his revelation of the post-earthly mission of Jesus.

INTERACT ONLINE

What new expressions of the church
(whether you call it that or not) have you experienced?

www.spencerburke.com/heretic/newexpressions

Jesus is the Tao

In his book *Living Buddha, Living Christ,* Thich Nhat Hanh forever changed my understanding of the Christian life when he spoke of Jesus as the Tao, the way.

To say that Jesus is the Tao is to acknowledge that the way he walked in the world is the path to follow. It is not about competing with other faith traditions. It's about living out a way of grace, love, forgiveness, and peace.

One of the verses in the Bible most quoted by Christians is found in John's gospel: "I am the way and the truth and the life. No one comes to the Father except through me." But what do those words really mean? Is Christianity truly the only right religion, the only truth?

Though often presented that way, I'm not sure it's really the case. When Jesus was talking about being the way, I don't think he was talking about religion. Religion as we understand it wasn't in his vocabulary. Although other faiths existed in Jesus' day, they were more toward the Greco-Roman paganism end of things, and given the context of this verse, it seems unlikely that that is the point Jesus was trying to make.

In Jesus' day, the competing ideologies were the violent politics of the zealots on one hand and the Pharisees' compromising attempts to curry favor and find positions of power on the other. When Jesus described himself as "the way," he seemed to be telling his followers that violence or conformity to other systems and structures is not the way to God. Instead, the way is found in the path he laid out.

Jesus didn't declare *Christianity* to be the way; no such thing yet existed. Besides, he already had a religion—his own Jewish faith. Yet he critiqued from the inside what he considered a faulty system, incapable of containing the fullness of God's grace. He could have said, "My version of a revised Judaism is the way," but he didn't. He said, "*I* am the way."

Some people hear me say that "Jesus is the Tao" and assume I must think all roads lead to heaven. I don't. I think God leads to God, and God is always bigger than our feeble attempts to contain God within the confines of our structures and systems.

In a similar vein, truth is not an abstract idea but a living person. It is not a question of making claims about Jesus as truth but rather one of experiencing the truth of who he is, outside the confines of a religious system. To claim that other religions are true only to the degree that their views of God are the same as Christian concepts is to make a claim that Jesus himself did not make.

The last claim Jesus made in this troublesome little verse in the book of John is perhaps the key to understanding the others: "I am the life." Jesus' life, not just his acts on our behalf but the life he lived on earth, is "the life." Living a life like Jesus' is what it truly means to live. Jesus declared his life to be the way to choose—not the way of zealotry or paganism or compromise, but a life committed to God, committed to God's ways, and committed to grace.

future church

Although I don't believe that the future of faith lies within the confines of institutional Christianity, I do want to offer some ideas about how the church might rethink its role in society and continue to contribute to the spiritual needs of the world.

In *Shalimar the Clown*, Salman Rushdie writes about one of the realities of life in the twenty-first century. "Everywhere is now part of everywhere else," he says. "Russia, America, London, Kashmir. Our lives, our stories, flow into one another's."

Rushdie's vision of a world interconnected and interdependent sets the tone for what the church must do to remain vital in the global community. It must first find its global soul. If it's true that the message of Jesus was never intended to be held captive behind the constructs of one particular interpretation, and if it's true that the church was only meant to help people find ways to live out Jesus' message of grace, then we have to find the boldness to come out from behind the walls.

The promiscuous Jesus

When Jesus first revealed himself as the Messiah, it was to an outsider—and a female outsider at that. The longest encounter between God and a woman in the entire Bible is recorded in the gospel of John, when Jesus stopped for water at a well. There he met a Samaritan woman, citizen of a nation the Jews regarded as outcasts, as explained in Chapter Two, for their heretical views about where and how God was to be worshiped. For the Jews, the Temple in Jerusalem was the only legitimate site for worship. The Samaritans, neighbors of the Jews and a people who, like the Jews, traced their ancestry back to the children of Jacob (later called Israel), insisted that they could worship on their own mountain. Because of the Samaritans' claim to legitimate genealogy and their refusal to worship only in Jerusalem, they represented division, if not outright heresy, for the Jews.

The story goes that Jesus had to go through Samaria on his way back to Galilee and stopped by a place called Jacob's Well for a drink. The symbolism of the place and the ethnic tensions surrounding the story are key to its contextual meaning in this story. A Samaritan woman comes to draw water from the well, and so begins a conversation between Jesus and an outsider. As both a Samaritan and a woman who had had five husbands, she was, as the author Jack Miles has pointed out, both a literal and figurative adulterer.

Drawing water was women's work, and a well was one of the few places women could be seen in public and talked to. "Will you give me a drink?" Jesus asks.

"You are a Jew and I am a Samaritan woman. How can you ask me for a drink?" she replies, stunned by his request.

"If you knew the generosity of God and who I am, you would be asking me for a drink, and I would give you fresh, living water," Jesus answers.

The woman tried to respond in a way that connected her both to the well and to Jacob who dug it. It was her way of saying that she already had a connection to God. She also jibes Jesus with the fact that he has no bucket to draw water, though the well was deep. Jesus tells her he was talking about a different kind of water that, once tasted, takes away thirst forever.

"Sir," she replies, "give me this water so that I won't get thirsty and have to keep coming here to draw water."

In what seems to be a strange shift in the conversation, Jesus then tells her to go and get her husband. Miles suggests that an undercurrent of flirtation and innuendo riddles this conversation. He points out that the play on words and metaphors are much like Shakespeare's use of words as swords and pricks in the beginning of *Romeo and Juliet*. Possibly detecting the flirtatious tone in the woman's voice, Jesus brings up the uncomfortable subject of her husband and asks her where he is. It turns out, of course, that she doesn't have one. Jesus rightly tells her that she has had five husbands and is not married to the man she is with at present.

In light of Jesus' insight into her life, the woman declares that Jesus must be a prophet and launches into a minisermon about how they are divided by religious perspectives. "Our fathers worshiped on this mountain, but you claim that the place where we must worship is in Jerusalem," she says. Again, Miles argues that she mentions this because "after upbraiding her for her marital infidelities, she expects that he will upbraid her nation for its religious promiscuity." But of course, Jesus doesn't. He gave no credence to either religion's view of the "right" way to worship. He does, however, reveal himself to her as the promised Messiah—something he had yet to do in the Jewish religious community or even among his own disciples in such specific language. But here, to an adulterous outsider, he reveals his purpose on earth, and the woman believes him.

Jesus' disciples, who had been away getting food, were surprised to find him talking to a woman when they return, but they leave the question of why he was talking with her unasked.

The story ends with Jesus telling the disciples to open their eyes and see that the fields "are ripe for harvest." This is the scandal of Jesus' "promiscuous" religion. It flirts with the world and offers grace—living water—to all.

Jesus' vision of God is not for the exclusive use of one community. It is not just for Jews or Christians or any other group. It is for anyone and everyone—Jewish, Christian, Buddhist, whatever. Jesus' encounter with a much-married woman is only one facet of this story. The real story, the real scandal, is Jesus' promiscuous view of God. Whatever role his religion expected him to play, Jesus ignored it and chose instead to forge a new path that included freedom for him to embrace everyone.

Advancing Beyond Atonement

Jesus didn't break the rules simply to be rebellious or contrary. He violated the Sabbath, healed the sick, welcomed the outcast, and reached out to those outside of Jewish faith because he was motivated by grace, the spirit of love, God's creative force. The religious community perceived Jesus' actions as a threat, but that was not his aim. His death was a consequence of those actions, not the intention behind them. The point of Jesus' life was not what he stood against but what he stood *for*, and he stood for life. When his existence is reduced (as some Christians believe) to the idea that he only lived to die, we miss the essence of who Jesus was.

One of the greatest sayings attributed to Jesus is "Greater love has no man than this, that a man lay down his life for his friends." The theme of sacrificial love is a redemptive theme found in classical literature and religious writings. Sacrificial love is central to the Judeo-Christian tradition and is expressed through a theological concept called atonement. Atonement seeks to capture the beauty of the idea of being reconnected with God.

> Atonement seeks to capture the beauty of the idea of being reconnected with god.

Many Christians advance the idea that Jesus' death was a way by which God satisfied God's own need for a punishment that could atone for the sins of the world and perpetuate the idea that God's willingness to punish Jesus on our behalf is what reveals God's love to us. The problem with this is that it leads to an overemphasis on putting faith in a God who loves us so much he is willing to sacrifice his son, and it can reinforce a caricature of a God who is angry, bloodthirsty, and judgmental. To balance this view, we need to act out in faith, living the way Jesus lived and standing up for the things he stood for. What counts is not a belief system but a holistic approach of following what you feel, experience, discover, and believe; it is a willingness to join Jesus in his vision for a transformed humanity.

For most of my Christian life, I have heard people say that it is not enough to do good works or care for the world. There has to

be faith in Jesus—which usually means assent to a set of proposi-
tions. But actually, the Apostle Paul said it is good works without
love—not good works without a belief system—that are empty and
worthless.

Moving forward, the institutional church has an opportunity
to broaden its view of Jesus and demonstrate true compassion in the
world.

Being the post office in an e-mail world

In my book *Making Sense of Church*, I offer seven metaphors for
churches to consider. These metaphors were meant as an encour-
agement to churches to view themselves differently, moving past
things like putting the emphasis on the Sunday event and seeing
themselves as the gatekeepers of eternity into new ways of gathering
and acting. The hope of the church, as I see it, is to take on a facilitating role, helping people find their way with God rather than
attempting to determine and control exactly what that relationship
to God "must" look like.

Since then, I've come up with a new word picture that sums
up the kind of role I see for the church in the future. Basically, I see
the institutional church as the post office in an e-mail world.

Remember when e-mail was first introduced? Everyone said
it would make the post office obsolete and probably save billions in
paper. It hasn't turned out that way, of course. The post office still
exists, and it still provides a valuable service. And as for paper, well,
we seem to be going through that resource quicker than ever as
everyone prints out their innumerable messages. Still, to be fair, the
role of the post office *is* greatly reduced.

There was a time when the post office was absolutely essential.
It was at the center of society. If you wanted to send a message to
someone or pay a bill, you needed a middleman—a letter carrier—

to do so. In the same way, the institutional church has long been the middleman between God and society.

In the past, the church was the center of the community. Its spires were visible for miles. In a world that wasn't literate, it was important for someone to read the Bible and interpret it. There was a demand for that service. The church was also a gathering place, a central location where you could find out what was going on in the world—who'd been sick, who died, who had a baby, who needed a meal, and so on. It was a connecting point. It offered services and insights you couldn't get anywhere else.

The world today is a vastly different place. The must-have Christmas gift for local teenagers this season was a Motorola Razr cell phone. It's a fantastic piece of technology, very sleek and futuristic-looking, but it's what the phone can do that excites teens today. It downloads music and movies, sends and receives e-mail, lets you surf the Web, and can be personalized with photos and ringtones.

A friend's teenage daughter spent much of Christmas day fielding calls from all her friends who got the same gift and programming the phone to her own tastes. It was almost comical to watch her with her laptop connected to the phone company's Web site, learning how to program the phone. She didn't even crack open the instruction book that came with the phone—she went straight to the Internet. Between the Internet and her phone, she now has a number of ways to communicate with her buddies— e-mail, instant messaging, Web cam, and voice mail. She chats constantly with friends from school and friends from camp who live all over the country; I doubt she has ever, ever sent a letter or a card to any of them. Well, not in the traditional manner, anyway. She is more "in touch" on a regular basis with her friends than her grandparents ever thought of being, and yet she uses none of what we would regard as traditional modes of communication. She is a child of the communication age, and electronic technology shapes her world. She does her homework on the computer, researching via Google and Wikipedia. The post office brings her the occasional piece of mail—a birthday card from a relative or a postcard from a friend unable to access the Internet, and every once in awhile a package. Apart from that, her life is lived out on a new communication network.

I am in no way saying that the postal system is obsolete. We still depend on it for many things, but increasingly, its role and function in our lives is being eclipsed by other means of information delivery. I can bank online and pay my bills from home any time of the day. I can communicate to friends all around the world in real time over the Internet, and I can send my parcels by any number of delivery services and choose one based on a number of personal issues such as price, time, and convenience. The post office just isn't the only option anymore. Not only are things decentralized today, but they're available on demand, at times that suit the user, not the system.

The challenge for people of faith who seek to move forward is to acknowledge these shifts in culture and recognize that the institutional church must now find its own way. The things people used to come to the one-hour event on Sunday morning for are not the drawing cards they once were. Today, it seems we respond directly to the mystery of the message that religion was created to decipher. We no longer need the systems of religion to find faith. We now live in a world where the sacred is beyond religion and the message of Jesus is transcending the institutional church.

The institutional church can dismiss this as a by-product of a consumer culture and insist that

> Today, it seems we respond directly to the mystery of the message that religion was created to decipher. We no longer need the systems of religion to find faith.

we need to get back to the basics. This could miss the point that "the basics" for a whole new generation have changed. Basic transportation is no longer a horse and buggy but a car. Basic education is not sixth-grade level but now demands at least some college credits. Basic religious instruction was once a sermon but is now multiple methods of communication.

A shared state of mind

Max Weber, the sociologist who defined the modern age as an "iron cage" ruled by bureaucrats and experts, said that social systems can be organized in three ways—by the sword, by the purse, or by the word. We experienced all of those attempts to organize ourselves through much of the twentieth century. Violence has never been far from our doorsteps as time and time again some figure—some Hitler or Stalin—rises up and attempts to rule by the sword. We have also seen the rise of the capitalist machine, where money shapes social values. Religions, of course, have used words, knowledge-based interpretations of text, in an attempt to move people in one di-. rection or another.

While all three of these forms of organization still function in one way or another, today the chief means of organizing seems to be emerging via information rather than knowledge-based systems. The Internet is allowing us to access and share information about everything—ideas, values, morals—in new ways, and it is reshaping the way we view ourselves as human beings. Moving forward, we must strive for a shared state of mind rather than for the superiority of any particular system. This means that we must celebrate difference, not simply tolerate it, and we must learn from one another.

It is possible today to get information about pretty much anything you are interested in. Things that were previously inaccessible can now be accessed and downloaded in a matter of minutes. Most of this information comes from outside of any "official" channels. It is posted and shared and commented on by interested parties. In a network system, information comes across the Web rather than from outside of it. It doesn't need a central organizing system.

Here comes Everybody

James Joyce, the Irish writer and poet, used the letters HCE—"here comes everybody"—numerous times in his final book, *Finnegan's Wake*. It was a literary device referring to the central character of his tale, and it occurred in many other ways throughout the story to describe a theme the author seemed to be trying to get at. For me, it points to Jesus' central message that his kingdom is open to anyone and everyone. "Here comes everybody" is a vision for a world united by God's grace, and it was "here comes everybody" thinking that got Jesus into trouble.

"There is neither Jew nor Greek, slave nor free, male nor female, for you are all one in Christ Jesus," wrote Paul in his letter to the Galatians. He wrote this in the context of a larger issue he was taking up with the Christians of that particular region. They had somehow become convinced that in order to truly follow Jesus, there needed to be some connection with Jewish faith and practice. They developed a formula that declared that Jesus *plus* Jewish tradition equaled salvation.

Understandably upset about this, Paul wrote to them in no uncertain terms that no requirements needed to be fulfilled to embrace God's gift of grace in Jesus. You don't need the law, Paul declared. You don't need certain holy days or festivals or human efforts. The Spirit of God starts us off on our journey with God, so why turn to our own efforts afterward? Paul went as far as to say that those who want to trust in religious law "are under a curse," because if one chooses to live under God's law, everything must be fulfilled to the letter. Since that is humanly impossible, you are in big trouble if you try!

"Live by the Spirit," said Paul, and things will go well for you. This is how Christian faith is meant to be expressed—not through legalistic systems of behavioral organization or by performing pre-scribed requirements. Paul's vision of Christian faith was a celebra-tion of diversity, an acknowledgment that differences exist, and a call to celebrate those differences within the horizons of Jesus' king-dom vision. The dean of Grace Cathedral in San Francisco, Alan Jones, wrote about his vision of grace beyond institutional religion.

> I am convinced that many long for an inclusive community
> that is liberating and not confining and in which they are allowed
> to think for themselves. I believe that a critical mass of people
> (though by no means the majority) long for a communion that is
> not authoritarian. And I do see a different kind of tribe emerging,
> one that doesn't eradicate tribal differences but celebrates them.

Jesus doesn't ask for universal agreement to a set of proposi-tions about himself. He simply invites us to follow him.

Born Again Again?

In John's gospel, Nicodemus, a leader of the Jews, comes to Jesus at night to ask some questions. He starts by stating that he knew Jesus had come from God—or he wouldn't have been able to teach and work miracles. Jesus replies to these comments in a strange way: "I tell you the truth, no one can see the kingdom of God unless he is born again."

Nicodemus doesn't get this concept at all. "How can a man be born when he is old?" Nicodemus asks. "Surely he cannot enter a second time into his mother's womb to be born!" Jesus tells him that there are two kinds of birth we can experience—one of the flesh and one of the spirit.

This passage has become part of the ammunition of institu-tional Christianity. "Come to Jesus. Be born again! Get involved in a Bible-believing church!" is the clarion call. But Jesus didn't actually tell Nicodemus he needed more religion or more dogma or more information. Nor did he tell him that he needed to be born again to get to heaven. What he did say is that everyone—Nicodemus included—needs to be born again in order to enter into the reign of God.

Nicodemus's story reminds us how easily our doctrines and religious formulations can overcomplicate the reality of God's love for us. One of Israel's theological leaders couldn't even grasp Jesus' words. To be born again, according to Jesus, is to commit oneself to the kingdom of God's purposes. It is to begin a journey with God in order to make the world a place of grace. It doesn't mean "getting religion"; it means committing ourselves to Jesus' vision of God's kingdom. What did Jesus say that is? In a word, love, plain and simple.

Jesus challenged Nicodemus's vision of an exclusive pious and religious community, which was in fact ignorant of the truth about how God truly saves the world. The Spirit is "like the wind," Jesus tells Nicodemus. "It blows wherever it wants to." We can hear wind and see its effects, but we have no idea where it comes from or where it is going. God's Spirit, like the wind, is not something we are meant to control. The Spirit as a wind starts us on a journey. We now learn to live, breathe, and walk in that way.

The Web journalist Tim Boucher put it another way. Religions, he wrote, are our attempt to "give form to the divine, because we suck at contemplating raw infinity." Religions are the

> nets which we cast in the hopes of catching god. But it's like trying to catch the sea with a net. It's much more likely that we'll just get ourselves tangled up, and god will slip through. I think god wants us to follow and imitate him as he playfully escapes our nets and challenges us to reach new levels of understanding and love.

Jesus called together a group of people in the gospels and invited them to join him in spreading the word to the world. In John's gospel, *love is* the word. Jesus saw a new kind of unity, a communion of people from all kinds of backgrounds coming together in a relational network based on love. Embracing this love sanctifies them, holding them together by a common experience of God's grace that causes them to respond to the world in a new way.

It is not about legalistic and rigid systems of belief. Jesus surrounded himself with a community of people whom the religious institutions looked down on—prostitutes, tax collectors, political seditionists, women, and children. He didn't condemn; he healed, restored, and encouraged. And he did this by violating religious and social norms—healing on the Sabbath, touching lepers and bleeding women—and particularly by not offering those in religious and secular positions of power the respect they assumed they deserved. He created his new community with the simple call, "Follow me, and I will make you fishers of men."   Jesus sought a community of difference made up of the least likely people one could imagine to be about God's business.

Another gospel story tells of an encounter between Jesus and a very wealthy young man determined to live a religious life. The young man comes to Jesus to ask what he needs to do to inherit "eternal life." Jesus replies that if he wants eternal life, he knows what to do, because the law of his religion tells him that he must keep the commandments. "All these I have kept," the man replies. "What do I still lack?"

Jesus' answer caused great consternation, not just for the young man but for pretty much everyone within earshot. "If you want to be perfect, go, sell your possessions and give to the poor, and you will have treasure in heaven. Then come, follow me." The young man wanted to live by the rules, depending on his observance of external obligations to guarantee him a spot in the afterlife. But Jesus had another vision and hit the man where it hurt, asking him to give up the one thing that mattered most to him—his wealth.

> Jesus' followers will find their way into the kingdom not by adhering to human standards . . . but by awakening to God's standards, based on grace.

He would rather hold on to what he perceived to be his safe and secure world of rules, traditions, and self-sufficiency than let go and simply follow Jesus. Jesus' kingdom is not based on external observances, which is why those who choose to follow him will find their way in the kingdom not by adhering to human standards, which is impossible, but by awakening to God's standards, based on grace.

A New Reading of the Text

When it comes to texts, the institutional church needs to let go of its rigid interpretations. Words—even in the Bible—are fluid and unstable, and their meanings shift and change. To insist that words in the Bible aren't fluid, though words used in other situations are, turns the Word of God into a legalistic and static document. "The letter kills," wrote Paul, "but the Spirit gives life." When metaphors become concrete and inflexible, they actually undermine the Christian view of God as alive and involved in our lives, because God is made to sound like a relic from a bygone age. The truth is that there have always been multiple interpretations of meaning in the Bible. The church has an opportunity to get away from an approach that turns Scripture into a hand-me-down version of religion and instead set free Jesus' words for a new generation.

A New Model of Leadership

Hope can also be found in embracing new ideas about leadership. It is fine to have a teacher as the ultimate leader if the model is educational. But the spiritual life is not simply about ingesting spoon-fed information. It is also about practice and participation. A new generation of leaders needs to emerge that recognizes this fact and can help all the different aspects of the "body," as Paul described the church in Corinthians, function well together.

A new kind of leader also has an opportunity to speak into the culture. For years, the more conservative and often extremist arms of the faith have functioned as caretakers. As a result, the church has been dismissed as full of bigots, homophobes, and aggressive conservatives. As Paul also said in Corinthians, we must beware of treating any part of the body as lesser or unimportant. We need to encourage a new kind of leader, one not afraid to challenge the present situation, to embrace and celebrate the unique and diverse talents of all the community, and to help us find a new voice to proclaim Jesus' message of grace.

Thinking Human, Thinking God

In a world as interconnected as ours, we must be aware of the impact our differences have on one another. Marshall McLuhan's vision of the world as a global village may be a bit of a stretch, but there is no doubt that we are connected to one another in ways that were inconceivable a couple of decades ago. The Internet has made it possible for all kinds of people to link themselves to a growing global community on the Web that exists outside space and time and outside of national and state boundaries. Old rules don't apply, and old wineskins won't work.

Global media bring the world into our living room. The whole world saw the tragedy of the Twin Towers, the devastation of the tsunami in Indonesia, the ravages and destruction of Hurricane Katrina, and the tragedy of the massive earthquake in Pakistan. We live those stories even though we are thousands of miles away from them. They have become the tragedies of our common humanity. They may happen far away, but we are increasingly aware that it could have been us and that in a sense it has happened to us.

We are also increasingly aware of the need to keep our aggressions in check. In an age of global terrorism, we need to cultivate a new sense of the sacredness of human life. We must think of the sacred as something related to what happens to us not only when we die but also in the here and now. We can't talk God without talking humanity. This is one focus of faith in the new millennium—to cultivate individuals and communities whose desire and commitment is to the common good. What we need is a "material" spirituality, a way of being in the world that treasures humanity in all its forms, celebrates the sacredness of all things, and walks in the Tao of Jesus.

spiritual Bricolage

Faith can be many things—an opinion, a compromise, a rediscovery, a revelation. Right now, faith is an experiment.

One of the most interesting things about living in an age of communication technology is the sheer availability of options and choices. We live in an age where there truly is never one answer to any question, whether it's about God or cornflakes! How we make sense of it all can be complicated. One of the ways people are navigating this new situation is by creating entirely new mixes of life. Everybody is engaged in the remixing of life. Just look at today's hiphop and rap music. Both genres are based on sampling bits and pieces of music from other sources and laying them over beats to create new songs. They sound familiar because they have echoes of other songs, mixed into brand-new songs. "Sampling is like sending a fax to yourself from the sonic debris of a possible future," says Paul Miller, a.k.a. DJ Spooky.

This approach can be helpful in thinking about how faith works in the new millennium. Sampling can be thought of as a form of *bricolage*, a French term for what a handyman does: tinkering at odd jobs, making and mending things from whatever bits and pieces are on hand, left over from other jobs. The philosopher Claude Lévi-Strauss used the word to describe the creation of new understandings of life from the bits and pieces of ideological thought that already exist. This is the clue to a new spiritual future. Spiritual bricolage is the mining of ideas and concepts about God that already exist in the world and creating a whole new vocabulary, as well as new concepts and understandings of what it means to have a spiritual life.

In contemporary culture, people are searching for words to describe all the shifts and changes they are going through, and the proliferation of new words is amazing. *Youniverse, gravanity*, and *massclusivity* are a few I have come across recently—attempts to describe subtle shifts in the global economy and the consumer's place in it. We also need a new spiritual vocabulary. Most people have to rely on words that no longer suffice for expressing their thoughts and feelings about the divine because these words have no replacements.

Some people have been using the term *technospirituality* lately to describe their own journey. It describes a spiritual life that is deeply interwoven with the new technologies that shape our world. Religion has always had its own language. Christians speak of redemption, justification, salvation, and so on. For many people today, the problem is not so much with the substance of faith but with the articulation of it. Old words no longer suffice, but new ones have not yet emerged.

A second element of faith today is related to the much older pastime of quilting. Quilting represents the communal aspect of contemporary spirituality. While bricolage helps us determine what is important to us and how faith can best inform and inspire our individual lives, quilting is about new ideas of community and gathering.

Making a quilt is a collaborative effort, with people coming together to create a beautiful blanket out of all the various bits and pieces of materials they bring to sew together. Quilting is the meeting of arts and crafts, both creative and functional. There are patterns for making traditional quilts, but there is also free rein to create a quilt of one's choosing. It simply requires that people work together to make something that benefits others. Likewise, the spiritual life is never lived in isolation, and individuality flourishes when community life nurtures it.

Here in the quilting realm, the church might find a place for itself. To revert to technological analogies for a moment, the church has been broadcast-oriented, functioning like a television network. On TV, all the channels are presented in order, with precise times given for the start of each program. If you want to watch a particular program, you need to know what channel it plays on and what time it begins. Churches are a bit like that. They have specific times their programming starts, and they list the topics that will be covered at those times. A church might plan a service on biblical principles for giving, and it doesn't really matter if it's the program of choice for its members, who may have other pressing needs.

The dominance of the broadcast model has been challenged in a number of ways recently. On a recent edition of Charlie Rose's program on PBS, Rose discussed many of these developments with Reed Hastings, the CEO of Netflix. TiVo, for instance, gives the viewer control of when and where to watch a particular show because it can be recorded and stored until it has been viewed. Other services like Netflix deliver movies to your door in one day and offer new ways to view films. The Internet is a connectivity model of organization, and it is this model to which the church must con-sider shifting. In contrast to a broadcast model, which simply sends information out through official channels whether it is needed or not, the Internet offers more user-friendly ways of connecting to information and people. "User-friendly" is not the best way to char-acterize the role of religion in society, but it hints at the idea. The Internet is an egalitarian tool that allows anyone and everyone access and opportunity to share and consume the things that interest them.

A secondary dynamic associated with a shift away from the broadcast model is the issue of control versus freedom. A broadcast model is all about control. The broadcast company assumes respon-sibility for the kind of programming available, whereas connectivity models allow for a greater freedom of choice and exposure. It will be a challenge for institutional Christianity to break out of the broadcast box and open new avenues for connectivity and commu-nity, but it is possible.

I'm also wary of "shrink-wrapping" these thoughts into a "new way of doing church." I realize that cultural context will play a large part in determining how much of this is applicable. Con-cepts about freedom are much more embedded in Western societies like the United States and Britain and might resonate more easily with institutional faiths there.

As always, this destabilization of institutional faiths can be seen as a threat or a blessing, as destruction or something good and necessary. We each have to make that determination for ourselves, but I am excited about the potential. This is not just theory—people are already putting these principles into practice. TheOOZE.com, an online community I started in 1998, is an attempt to shift to a connectivity mode by allowing people from diverse backgrounds to come together and communicate with each other.

Think about it this way. A woman in Africa sets up an Inter-net business with a small loan, a solar-powered laptop, and a cell phone. She connects to eBay and puts her handcrafted baskets up for sale. DHL picks up her products and delivers them anywhere in the world. PayPal completes the transactions, and money is deposited in her local account. Perhaps her husband is upset because she is no longer fulfilling her duties and obligations according to tribal tradition, but her work is generating more income to lift her family out of poverty, and she can pay for education for her children.

Yes, things are changing, and I believe they are changing for the better. The seeds of a new social order are developing—an order that offers more equality, more hope, and more of a future than was conceivable just a few short years ago.

Perhaps the same is true for institutional faiths that are willing to shift from the broadcast mode into the more egalitarian world of interconnectivity. What is lost is the exclusive sound of one's own voice. What is gained is the opportunity to be heard.

on Beyond zebra

Theodor Geisel, better known as Dr. Seuss, was a prolific storyteller whose tales such as *The Cat in the Hat* and *Green Eggs and Ham* are loved by people of all ages. His stories are unique on so many levels—postmodern morality tales, told in a rhythm and poetry of his own making. One of my favorite Dr. Seuss books is *On Beyond Zebra*. It is about words, language, and alphabets, and it captures all I have been saying about what it might take to create a faith for the future.

> Said Conrad Cornelius o'Donald o'Dell,
> My very young friend who is learning to spell:
> "The A is for Ape. And the B is for Bear.
> The C is for Camel. The H is for Hare.
> The M is for Mouse. And the R is for Rat.

I know *all* the twenty-six letters like that. . . .
So now I know everything anyone knows
From beginning to end. From the start to the close.
Because Z is as far as the alphabet goes. . . ."
Then he almost fell flat on his face on the floor
When I picked up the chalk and drew one letter more!
A letter he never had dreamed of before!
And I said, "*You* can stop, if you want, with the Z
Because most people stop with the Z
But not me!
In the places I go there are things that I see
That I *never* could spell if I stopped with the Z.
I'm telling you this 'cause you're one of my friends.
My alphabet starts where *your* alphabet ends!"

In the past, institutions wanted to put their seal of approval on everything. It is like the movie *The Truman Show*, where what one man thinks is his real life turns out to be, in fact, a carefully crafted and orchestrated reality television show. Nothing is real, and everything is carefully branded. Institutions function a lot like that at times. They want to make sure that their mark is carried on every product and that life is a well-orchestrated machine. This is why there are Christian radio and television stations, theme parks, clothes, bookstores, musicians, and just about everything else.

But Truman, the central character of *The Truman Show*, walked away from this carefully crafted and branded world once he realized he could contribute to his own future. The television company's control over his life was forever broken, because life is too precious to live under the weight of somebody else's opinion of what it should look like.

In moving into the world of material spirituality, the world of bricolage and quilting, institutional faiths like Christianity have the opportunity once again to offer their threads of what a life with God can be and return to their real purpose—not controlling the gates of heaven but facilitating new life in the people who encounter faith and grace.

SECTION III

Living in Grace

Mystical Responsibility

Jesus the Heretic

The Word became flesh and
made his dwelling among us . . .
full of grace and truth.

—John 1:14

In this last section of the book, I want to focus on the implications of grace for each of us on a personal level. One expression sums it up best: "Sometimes you gotta break the rules."

When I used to teach photography, students would become frustrated at spending class after class covering the basics of composition and point of view and learning about fundamental camera operations like f-stops and shutter speeds. But there was a method to my madness. We practiced these lessons until they became almost second nature to the students, who were then able to create images without having to struggle with the technical aspects of their photography.

Once the students were so comfortable with the techniques and had worked through their initial desire for self-expression, I gave them a new assignment: break at least two rules in creating their next image. After spending so much time learning the fundamentals, they were shocked that I was now inviting them to violate those rules. But no sooner had I given the assignment than the students began to buzz with creativity. They were excited about interpreting their surroundings in new ways, and the weekly critiques moved from objective evaluation to lively dialogue. The students could now identify why a photograph was original, imaginative, and unique because they could see the tension and beauty that came from breaking the rules—with intent.

At the end of the semester, students displayed their portfolios of work before the class. Although the proficiency and technical excellence of the students' earlier works was impressive, it was always the photos from the end of the semester that captured the eye and imagination of the viewers. It was amazing to watch students who had initially signed up for the course merely to receive credit move into a new world of self-expression and personal enjoyment. They went beyond competing for a grade to become collaborators and collectors of one another's work.

I think now is an excellent time to break the rules of religion and institutional faith in a similar way. But here's the thing: I don't think we should break away from tradition just to make a point; I think we should do it . . . because Jesus did.

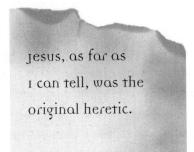

Jesus, as far as I can tell, was the original heretic.

People have accused me over the years of not paying enough attention to Scripture or not being "in the Word" enough. But the truth is that I have these crazy thoughts about love and grace and all the rest precisely because I *do* read the Bible. And Jesus, as far as I can tell, was the original heretic.

The clichés of our forebears

Some time later, Jesus went up to Jerusalem for a feast of the Jews. Now there is in Jerusalem near the Sheep Gate a pool, which in Aramaic is called Bethesda and which is surrounded by five covered colonnades. Here a great number of disabled people used to lie—the blind, the lame, the paralyzed. One who was there had been an invalid for thirty-eight years. When Jesus saw him lying there and learned that he had been in this condition for a long time, he asked him, "Do you want to get well?"

"Sir," the invalid replied, "I have no one to help me into the pool when the water is stirred. While I am trying to get in, someone else goes down ahead of me."

Then Jesus said to him, "Get up! Pick up your mat and walk." At once the man was cured; he picked up his mat and walked.

The day on which this took place was a Sabbath, and so the Jews said to the man who had been healed, "It is the Sabbath; the law forbids you to carry your mat."

But he replied, "The man who made me well said to me, 'Pick up your mat and walk.'"

So they asked him, "Who is this fellow who told you to pick it up and walk?"

The man who was healed had no idea who it was, for Jesus had slipped away into the crowd that was there.

Later Jesus found him at the temple and said to him, "See, you are well again. Stop sinning or something worse may happen to you." The man went away and told the Jews that it was Jesus who had made him well.

So because Jesus was doing these things on the Sabbath, the Jews persecuted him. Jesus said to them, "My Father is always at his work to this very day, and I, too, am working." For this reason, the Jews tried all the harder to kill him; not only was he breaking the Sabbath, but he was even calling God his own Father, making himself equal with God.

In the story from John's gospel, Jesus healed a man who was an invalid for almost forty years. Jesus had healed before, but never on the Sabbath. For the Jews, the Sabbath was a holy day. "Remember the Sabbath by keeping it holy" is one of the Ten Commandments that shaped the religion of the Jews. The Sabbath was traditionally a commemoration of the seventh day of Creation, when God ceased laboring and rested. Followers of God were told to do likewise and rest from their labors on the Sabbath. Some Jews were so committed to keeping the Sabbath that they created a complex series of laws and prohibitions to make sure no one broke the law against working. In fact, by the time of Jesus, the Jews had identified more than six hundred infractions that could be incurred on the Sabbath. It was almost impossible to move without violating some detail of Sabbath law.

Jesus violated the Sabbath with intention. He knew what it represented, knew the rules governing his religion, yet he still chose to act. He could have waited until the rules permitted such action. Doctors were permitted to work to save the life of someone in danger, but the man Jesus healed had been an invalid for thirty-eight years. Let's be real—the guy wasn't going anywhere. What would it matter if Jesus waited one more day to heal him?

The man himself even seemed a little resistant to Jesus, almost as if Jesus' question of whether he wanted to be healed was from so far out in left field that he didn't know how to respond. He told Jesus he had no one to help him get into the pool, which meant he had no hope of healing. Tradition said an angel would occasionally come and stir the waters of the pool. The first person then into the waters would be healed. It must have been a sad situation, all those sick people waiting for a chance at healing, knowing they had to be ready at any moment to get into the water. You can only imagine the sense of competition in the air.

Into this scene of human despair Jesus came one Sabbath to perform not an act of rebellion but a creative act designed to generate a new vision of the life of faith. Jesus healed the invalid—and then, by making him carry his mat out with him, brought him under scrutiny of the religious authorities who were monitoring the people for the slightest infraction of the law, as religious people often do.

When the religious authorities finally confronted Jesus about his Sabbath violations, he refuted the idea that God doesn't work on the Sabbath. "My Father is always at his work," said Jesus. Maybe God rested on that first Sabbath, but God doesn't rest every Sabbath. Jesus reasoned that if God works on the Sabbath, then so may his followers. Though completely logical, this statement only angered the leaders even more because Jesus presumed to know the inside scoop on God's activity beyond what Moses had revealed to the Jews.

A little later in John's story, the issue of healing the man on the Sabbath was raised once again and Jesus expanded his answer a bit more.

> "I did one miracle, and you are all astonished. Yet because Moses gave you circumcision [though actually it did not come from Moses, but from the patriarchs], you circumcise a child on the Sabbath. Now if a child can be circumcised on the Sabbath so that the law of Moses may not be broken, why are you angry with me for healing the whole man on the Sabbath? Stop judging by mere appearances, and make a right judgment."

Jesus argued that the Pharisees had no trouble finding a way around the Sabbath when they wanted to inscribe their religious beliefs into someone else's life. But restoring a man to full health violated the law? Perhaps Jesus just wanted to embarrass the religious leaders. After all, who could really get upset when another human being finds health and wholeness again?

But therein lies the folly of our religious institutions. Their

our views of what is right become corrupted when we believe that we have a clear and complete understanding of the nature and character of god.

laws become hindrances to the expression of full humanity. Our views of what is right become corrupted when we believe that we have a clear and complete understanding of the nature and character of God.

For the religious authorities of Jesus' time, like those of most religions, it was all about observances of rules, regulations, days, dates, and festivals. All these things took precedence over human need and acts of compassion. "The greatest enemy of truth is very often not the lie—deliberate, contrived, and dishonest," said John F. Kennedy. Instead, it is the "myth—persistent, persuasive, and realistic. Too often we hold fast to the clichés of our forebears." The legalistic perception of what was important distorted their relationship with God. They had forgotten that deep within their religious history had been the call to reach beyond themselves in compassion. "The Lord is compassionate and gracious, slow to anger, abounding in love," one of the Old Testament poets wrote.

The author Douglas Rushkoff has said that religion has two main functions but usually winds up focusing on only one of them. Religion is a form of social control, helping keep our baser tendencies in check and preventing violent and destructive people from harming others. But religion is also meant to inspire thinking and help people achieve new levels of understanding and spiritual development. Rushkoff argues that religions usually opt for the former, seeking to control the masses. This might work in the short term, Rushkoff contends, but ultimately it promotes a "blind faith in a set of rules for moral behavior, established not by God but by whoever happens to be in charge."

This is what Jesus rejected with every ounce of his being. He had no time for religion that precluded and prevented acts of compassion for the broken and hurting, no matter the day of the week.

writing in the dust

At dawn [Jesus] appeared again in the temple courts, where all the people gathered around him, and he sat down to teach them.

The teachers of the law and the Pharisees brought in a woman caught in adultery. They made her stand before the group and said to Jesus, "Teacher, this woman was caught in the act of adultery. In the Law Moses commanded us to stone such women. Now what do you say?" They were using this question as a trap, in order to have a basis for accusing him.

But Jesus bent down and started to write on the ground with his finger. When they kept on questioning him, he straightened up and said to them, "If any one of you is without sin, let him be the first to throw a stone at her." Again he stooped down and wrote on the ground.

At this, those who heard began to go away one at a time, the older ones first, until only Jesus was left, with the woman still standing there. Jesus straightened up and asked her, "Woman, where are they? Has no one condemned you?"

"No one, sir," she said.

"Then neither do I condemn you," Jesus declared. "Go now and leave your life of sin."

Sex and sexual sins were complicated in biblical times. Laws about sexuality often had different implications for men and women. Take, for example, the laws regarding adultery. If a married man had sex with an unmarried woman, it was not considered adultery, but if a married woman had sex with anyone other than her husband, she had committed adultery, and the law required that she be stoned to death if she was caught. The only time a similar fate awaited a man was if he had sex with a woman who was married or engaged to someone else.

A person could not be convicted of adultery based on circumstantial evidence. It had to be witnessed, which was what occurred in this particular situation. A suspicious husband could, however, bring his wife before a religious leader and require her to drink the "water of bitterness," water mixed with dust from the temple floor. If she was guilty, the theory was that God would "strike her thigh"—give her abdominal pains—until she confessed, falling, of course, under the curse against adultery and becoming subject to death.

Adultery was first and foremost viewed as an offense against God. This is why adultery and apostasy (the renunciation of faith in God) were so closely linked in the Old Testament. Against this backdrop, Jesus thus found himself drawn into a challenging conversation when the adulterous woman was brought before him.

A lot of drama surrounds this story; it must have been tense. Jesus seemed to spend most of the time not looking at anyone but writing on the ground instead. A lot of people have conjectured about what he was writing and why, but the story doesn't tell us. We do know that the religious leaders were using this situation to try to trap Jesus, and so they asked him what he thought should be done, knowing full well what the law demanded and what any believer worth his salt would say. But as usual, Jesus didn't give them the answer they expected. In fact, it's perhaps what he didn't say that stands out. Jesus never condemned the woman—not even after everyone else left. Jesus' admonishment to leave her sinful ways behind can almost be read as good common sense as much as a comment on sin—like saying, "This is what happens when you get caught with your pants down, and so I'd avoid this kind of thing in the future if I were you."

What Jesus did do was set a new standard of mercy for God. God's justice had never faltered before. In the Old Testament, God is proclaimed as "merciful and gracious, slow to anger, and abounding in steadfast love and faithfulness," but the same passage also declares that God does not let any sin slide and metes out a singular form of justice that affects even the great-grandchildren of wrongdoers. In contrast, the adulteress got none of this from Jesus. Instead, she got to walk away, free from guilt and shame.

The religious leaders didn't get the message that God was now in the mercy business, so they assumed that stoning was still the way to go, and they expected Jesus to concur. But of course, he didn't because his vision of God was not like theirs.

Perhaps the image of Jesus writing in the dust reminds us that we are dust, blown away by the wind and incapable of fully realizing the scope of God's grace. Perhaps it is also a reminder that rather than seeking to etch our concepts in stone, we should write them in the dust so that they can always be rewritten as we grow in grace and love.

Rowan Williams, the current archbishop of Canterbury, was in a church not far from the World Trade Center in New York City on September 11, 2001. After being trapped in such a vulnerable place, seeing the horror of the terrorist attacks with his own eyes, and finding himself covered with the dust of that terrible tragedy, he wrote a book about how he felt a Christian might respond to all the challenges raised by such a terrible thing. One of the things we ought to resist, he argued, is the tendency of "using other people to think with," meaning that it's dangerous to use other people as symbols for our view of the world, imposing our personal opinions and perspectives on another person's life. The religious leaders who dragged this poor woman, naked and ashamed, before Jesus, used her, in effect, as a "person to think with," their reference point for how God deals with human brokenness. She became in their hands a nonperson, a trap to capture Jesus, and it backfired.

Archbishop Williams's book, *Writing in the Dust*, closes with a thought about this story and the dust Jesus wrote in: "He does not draw a line, fix an interpretation, tell the woman who she is and what her fate should be. He allows a moment, a longish moment, in which people are given time to see themselves differently precisely because he refuses to make the sense they want. When he lifts his head there is both judgment and release." The judgment is against all who want to make God, first and foremost, a judge and condemner of humanity. The release is for those bruised by life, by their own foolishness, yet who receive mercy and grace from God.

This story represents a shift in God's character—or, if it makes you more comfortable, a change in our perception of God's character. Either way, if God or the perception of God had changed, the Jews could not remain unchanged. The problem was that they wanted to stay the same. This was the dilemma Jesus created among them. "We know you are a teacher who has come from God," Nicodemus says in the book of John. But the unspoken issue was that by acknowledging that Jesus came from God, the Jews either had to make him conform to and affirm their ways or had to shift their thinking to embrace his new theology. They preferred the former, which, of course, didn't work because Jesus didn't come to conform to conventional standards of God's kingdom.

A New Ethic for God's People?

On one occasion an expert in the law stood up to test Jesus. "Teacher," he asked, "what must I do to inherit eternal life?"

"What is written in the Law?" he replied. "How do you read it?"

He answered: "'Love the Lord your God with all your heart and with all your soul and with all your strength and with all your mind'; and, 'Love your neighbor as yourself.'"

"You have answered correctly," Jesus replied. "Do this and you will live."

But he wanted to justify himself, so he asked Jesus, "And who is my neighbor?"

In reply Jesus said: "A man was going down from Jerusalem to Jericho, when he fell into the hands of robbers. They stripped him of his clothes, beat him and went away, leaving him half dead. A priest happened to be going down the same road, and when he saw the man, he passed by on the other side. So too, a Levite, when he came to the place and saw him, passed by on the other side. But a Samaritan, as he traveled, came where the man was; and when he saw him, he took pity on him. He went to him and bandaged his wounds, pouring on oil and wine. Then he put the man on his own donkey, took him to an inn and took care of him. The next day he took out two silver coins and gave them to the innkeeper. 'Look after him,' he said, 'and when I return, I will reimburse you for any extra expense you may have.'

"Which of these three do you think was a neighbor to the man who fell into the hands of robbers?"

The expert in the law replied, "The one who had mercy on him."

Jesus told him, "Go and do likewise" (Luke 10:25–37).

There are many layers to this story. We have already talked about Samaritans and the Jews' low regard of them. For Jesus, as a Jew, to make a Samaritan the hero of this tale was at least an affront to the Jewish sensibilities, if not a downright slap in the face. Another issue in this story is the identity of the man who was robbed and beaten. A faithful Jew who touched the body of an outsider violated the Law and became contaminated, requiring a lengthy purification rite.

But there is something else. Jesus told this story in response to a question posed by a religious expert who asked Jesus for a definition of "neighbor" in light of God's command to "love your neighbor as yourself." Jesus' definition of a "neighbor" seems to be "anyone you come across," but this was not the definition the Jews were used to. In Leviticus, a neighbor is clearly defined as someone you know, from your own people. In context, the command reads, "Do not seek revenge or bear a grudge against one of your people, but love your neighbor as yourself." Consequently, there seems to be a lot of possible justification there for avoiding someone one couldn't immediately identify as a neighbor.

In expanding the definition of who is a neighbor, Jesus said there is no distinction between Jews and their neighbors based on genetics and ethnicity. This was a revolutionary and incendiary idea. The Jews had lived for centuries with the sense of being God's chosen and privileged people, and now Jesus dared to alter that? It struck at the very heart of what it meant to be Jewish. Their uniqueness had led to the creation of all kinds of rules and regulations about keeping separate from everything and everyone declared unclean. Their whole religion was built on purity codes and the idea of separation. And here Jesus turned it inside out—or did he? Perhaps he was simply clarifying something that had been fuzzy for too long. He said that it is no longer ethnicity but ethics that separate. Jesus' vision of God's kingdom was made up not of one particular group of people but rather of all peoples who will gladly respond in mercy and compassion to the strangers they meet. Jesus established the idea that God, not God's people, determines who is of God and who is not.

INTERACT ONLINE
After reading some of these stories,
do you think Jesus was a heretic or not?

www.spencerburke.com/heretic/Jesusheretic

Talking About an Evolution

"You have heard that it was said to the people long ago, 'Do not murder, and anyone who murders will be subject to judgment.' But I tell you that anyone who is angry with his brother will be subject to judgment. . . .

"You have heard that it was said, 'Do not commit adultery.' But I tell you that anyone who looks at a woman lustfully has already committed adultery with her in his heart. . . .

"It has been said, 'Anyone who divorces his wife must give her a certificate of divorce.' But I tell you that anyone who divorces his wife, except for marital unfaithfulness, causes her to become an adulteress, and anyone who marries the divorced woman commits adultery.

"Again you have heard that it was said to the people long ago, 'Do not break your oath, but keep the oaths you have made to the Lord.' But I tell you, do not swear at all: either by heaven, for it is God's throne; or by the earth, for it is his footstool. . . . Simply let your 'Yes' be 'Yes,' and your 'No,' 'No'. . . .

"You have heard that it was said, 'Eye for eye, and tooth for tooth.' But I tell you, do not resist an evil person. If someone strikes you on the right cheek, turn to him the other also. . . .

"You have heard that it was said, 'Love your neighbor and hate your enemy.' But I tell you, love your enemies and pray for those who persecute you, that you may be sons of your Father in heaven."

In what feels like a very early prototype of a Dr. Seuss book, Jesus embarked on an *On Beyond Rules* journey here in the Sermon on the Mount. Taking the very essence of Jewish religious identity contained in these ancient stipulations, Jesus redrew the canvas of spiritual life and painted a picture of something so deep, so profound, and so beyond mere religious regulations that it has continued to capture the imaginations of readers for thousands of years. Those who like Jesus but resist Christianity often cite the Sermon on the Mount. Many of my friends bring it up when a conversation turns to belief as a model for the kind of person they want to be and the sort of life they desire to live. It has inspired everyone from Martin Luther King Jr. to Mahatma Gandhi.

Jesus didn't rewrite the rule book. He threw it out and exchanged it for a new way of being in the world. Not murdering someone is not enough, Jesus said. Few of us would even consider that anyway. But we all have anger and rage and jealousy, so let's deal with that and live in kindness toward each other.

In these few verses, Jesus initiated a revolution in human consciousness that exchanged good behavior for compassionate living. It exchanged human violence for a spiritual life grounded in the love and goodness of God on a level never before experienced in the world. Jesus shifted the religious conversation beyond the prescriptive that characterized the faith he grew up with, reached down into the soul of God, and drew up something so profound that when he was finished, all the people gathered "were amazed at his teaching, because he taught as one who had authority, and not as their teachers of the law."

Jesus' authority was not drawn from the long tradition that the teachers of the law drew from. His was a *new* power and authority introducing new practices, a new way of living that seemed to come out of nowhere. Of course, it came from God's Spirit, on which Jesus' life was entirely dependent, and not from the faith tradition. In Luke's gospel, which contains a version of the Sermon on the Mount, Luke described Jesus going into his local synagogue and declaring, "The Spirit of the Lord is on me" (Luke 4:18). This occurred right after Jesus had spent forty days in the desert wrestling with the devil and resisting the religious path as a means of achieving his aims and desires.

All you need is love

"I tell you the truth, one of you is going to betray me."

His disciples stared at one another, at a loss to know which of them he meant.

One of them, the disciple whom Jesus loved, was reclining next to him. Simon Peter motioned to this disciple and said, "Ask him which one he means."

Leaning back against Jesus, he asked him, "Lord, who is it?"

Jesus answered, "It is the one to whom I will give this piece of bread when I have dipped it in the dish." Then, dipping the piece of bread, he gave it to Judas Iscariot, son of Simon. As soon as

Judas took the bread, Satan entered into him.

"What you are about to do, do quickly," Jesus told him, but no one at the meal understood. . . .

When [Judas] was gone, Jesus said, "Now is the Son of Man glorified and God is glorified in him. If God is glorified in him, God will glorify the Son in himself, and will glorify him at once.

"My children, I will be with you only a little longer. You will look for me, and just as I told the Jews, so I tell you now: Where I am going, you cannot come.

"A new command I give you: Love one another. As I have loved you, so you must love one another. By this all men will know that you are my disciples, if you love one another."

In the face of betrayal, Jesus gave his followers a new command to love one another, just as he loved them in the midst of Judas's betrayal. And it wasn't just Judas who betrayed Jesus. *None* of the disciples seemed to know if he was the one. It was as if, at any given moment, any of them could have collapsed under the pressure and sold Jesus down the river. Later that same night, most of them did.

Once again, Jesus changed the playing field. Where the law produced judgments for those who betrayed God, Jesus produced love as betrayal's remedy. Whether or not you believe Jesus is God is not important to this story. The fact is that Jesus assumed a "God posture" and defined a code for *his* followers to live by. Love in the face of betrayal. Love in the face of disappointment and loss. This is what is written in stone for those who would follow Jesus. The Jews were identified by their commitment to live by the regulations of law: "Thou shalt" or "Thou shalt *not*." Jesus transformed a covenant of law into a community of love.

Later the same night, the rest of the disciples ran off and left Jesus alone to face his accusers. Even Peter, Jesus' most verbal supporter, finally denied him. But true to his own command, Jesus showed nothing but love and eventually brought all the disciples back into his embrace.

"Love cancels what betrayal causes," wrote Ray Anderson in his wonderful book *The Gospel According to Judas*. The book is a conversation between Jesus and Judas about the limits of God's love—or perhaps I should say the limitless love of God. Using imaginary dialogue between Jesus and Judas, Anderson wove a wonderful vision of God's love. Broken by his betrayal, Judas saw no hope for himself, but Jesus offered this: "We can never return to our innocence. But the love that has suffered loss is not a crippled love: it can be healed and made a stronger love."

Judas was overwhelmed by this response and said that his betrayal went beyond denial and unfaithfulness and "burned the bridge that made their relationship possible."

Jesus' reply echoes what John tells us in his gospel: "There never was a way back," Anderson explains. "There is only a way forward. The past can only be returned to us out of the future. Love is greater than faith and hope, because it can heal faithlessness and cure hopelessness."

> jesus rooted god firmly in the world, not only in the distant heavens, and he made human relationships the context in which god can be experienced.

This command to love that Jesus inaugurated reveals something about God that has been veiled by religion's dependence on rules. It declares that God is not external and detached, passively watching to make sure all the rules are kept. Instead, God is a *relational* presence, connecting with people via love, not regulation. Jesus rooted God firmly in the world, not only in the distant heavens, and he made human relationships the context in which God can be experienced. We make our connection with God by the love we show for each other.

Upon these revolutionary ideas, Jesus initiated his vision for a new way of being with God and others in the world. It wasn't just an alternative take on religion. It was the voicing of a new world. It was heretical in the eyes of many, and religion did what it generally does when its view of the universe is threatened. It tried to hold him down. But it couldn't.

The inquisitions

The term inquisition refers to a number of historical movements initiated by the Catholic church in an attempt to suppress heresies over a span of 750 years. The four major inquisitions began in 1184 with the Episcopal Inquisition and ended with the abolishment of the Spanish Inquisition in 1834.

In 1184, a papal bull—an official letter from the pope—established the first inquisition. Titled *Ad abolendam*—"for the purpose of doing away with"—it targeted the growing Catharist heresy in France. The Cathars were a group of Christians who believed that God had made only eternity perfect and that the material world was created by the devil. Consequently, they shunned fancy food, marriage, and wealth, practicing strict asceticism. Because it was administered by local bishops (*episcopus* is the Latin word for bishop), this first inquisition earned the title of the Episcopal Inquisition.

The second inquisition began in the 1230s in response to the failure of the previous inquisition and, by decree of the pope, was run by people trained specifically for the task. Individuals and clergy were chosen from different religious orders, but those from the

Dominican order made up the majority. The Dominicans had a long history of combating heresy, were good at arguing, and were well educated. Their monastic order also required a vow of poverty, so they were not prone to accepting bribes.

King Ferdinand and Queen Isabella of Castile founded the Spanish Inquisition in 1478. Largely run by the monarchs, only the chief inquisitor was appointed by the pope. The Spanish Inquisition represented a particularly brutal period in the history of the church, with countless Muslims, Jews, and "wayward" Christians brutalized by torture and violence.

In an attempt to duplicate the success of the Spanish Inquisition, King João III of Portugal initiated the final inquisition in 1536. It was finally abolished in 1821.

Alongside these inquisitions, Pope Paul III established a permanent office in the church in 1542 to maintain and defend the integrity of the faith and to examine and deal with errors of teaching and false doctrines. Known as the Congregation for the Doctrine of the Saints, it was led by Cardinal Joseph Alois Ratzinger from 1981 until his election as Pope Benedict XVI in 2005.

The Mystery
of God,
Grace, and
salvation

Have you seen that show on TV where a team of professional organizers comes in and helps people conquer the messiest rooms in their homes? It's fascinating to watch. Over the course of forty-eight hours, families pare down their belongings to only the essentials. Everything has to go in one of three piles: keep, sell, or throw out.

First of all, I'm always amazed at the stuff people keep, but more than that, it's amazing to see how *attached* people are to their things. I'm reminded of that clip of Charlton Heston at the National Rifle Association convention a few years ago, holding a gun over his head and saying, "From my cold, dead hands"—only in this case the sacred items range from wedding dresses and old stuffed animals to high school football jerseys. That's where the professionals come in, of course. Their job is to talk sense into people and help them see their objects for what they are—objects.

The truth is that sometimes we have to let go of things in our lives, however comforting they may be, and we need people to help us do it. In this chapter, I want to highlight some of the concepts of

God that have shaped me over the years but no longer fit the way they used to. Having addressed the issues I see with religion and the institutional church in earlier chapters, I want to turn now to the personal level.

somewhere out there

The big guy. The man upstairs. The big kahuna. The world is filled with thousands of different takes on precisely who and what God is, but the idea of God as a sort of huge, humanlike being sitting on a throne has been around for years.

As a pastor, I used to ask people to describe God to me, and it was always fascinating to hear the things they'd say. When things were going well and life was treating them well, God was often described as a grandfatherly figure—a kind soul who made things happen with a wink and a smile. At other times, people pictured God as Scrooge—a mean old man who was quick to judge and a stickler for details. Still others saw God as a kind of superhero. He might look ordinary enough on the outside, but make him mad, and he just might throw down a lightning bolt or two.

Does it matter how we conceive of God? I think it does. The singer Nick Cave's song "Into My Arms" provides wonderful insight into the power of love to transform the heart, but it's also a theological commentary. "I don't believe in an interventionist God, / But I know, darling, that you do," it begins. Cave goes on to say that if he did believe in that kind of God, he would want God to stay away from their romance and not touch a hair on his lover's head, or, if God did get involved, he would only want God to drive her into Cave's arms. How we perceive God can affect the way we live out our religions *and* our lives. It's not just how we picture God that matters but where God is in relation to us.

The idea of God being somewhere else has long been a Christian view. The language of both the Old and New Testaments would seem to support this perspective. "As the Father has sent me, I am sending you," Jesus says in John's gospel, or "Our Father who is in heaven," as we read in the Lord's Prayer. The language evokes the idea of distance and implies that God is doing the sending from some other place. This idea of God being somewhere else has a technical name, *transcendence*, which means existence apart and above the material world.

When the universe was a much smaller place, as it was in the days before Copernicus, the idea that God was somewhere else was an entirely different prospect. Medieval drawings of the universe, such as Dante's geometric drawings of the many levels of heaven and hell, have a framework that captures both the distance and closeness of God. Sure, God might be somewhere else, but God is not far away, because the whole universe is centered on the earth, and heaven, where God dwells, is right above us.

But the modern age changed that perspective, albeit unintentionally. The dawn of the age of science, and the embrace of scientific rationalism as a way of knowing the world, created more distance between humanity and God. As science took over the role of explaining the natural world,

As science took over the role of explaining the natural world, god was effectively pushed out of the universe.

God was effectively pushed out of the universe, and the distance between the divine and humanity became even greater.

Around this time, new theological views developed to explain the new relationship between God and the universe. One of them was deism, a view that some of the Founding Fathers—Thomas Jefferson, John Adams, and others—advocated. They rejected things like the miracle stories in the Bible and attempted to find more rational explanations for them. Deists basically believed God was involved in the initial creation of the world but then stepped back and let things run on their own. God was like a watchmaker who winds a clock and then leaves it alone. This view placed God even further away, in the backwaters of the universe, far from the lives of enlightened humanity.

Among people clinging to a more "Christian" view of things, God was still thought to be all-powerful and active in the world and human affairs, in spite of the distance. God was like Nick Cave's "interventionist God," occasionally breaking into our world to perform a miracle or bring a disaster, all the while supposedly compassionately and lovingly engaged in the lives of his people.

The great challenge to this view of God arrived in the twentieth century, because if God truly was "out there" and yet still intervened in the affairs of humanity, then where was he in a century of incredible human evil and destruction? Why didn't God intervene in the Holocaust or any of the other great tragedies of what some say was the bloodiest century in the history of humanity? And if God was all-powerful, loving, and compassionate, where was that power, love, and compassion when it was most needed?

if we maintain the concept of a metaphysical god ruling from the heavens, the world will continue to feel as if it is spinning out of control.

Ideas of God change slowly, and in spite of a quantum shift in the way we understand ourselves and the universe around us, many people still believe that God is somewhere "out there." People around the world continue to connect personal losses and national disasters with the sudden act of an angry and interventionist God.

The other end of the theological spectrum concerns God's closeness—*immanence* is the technical term, meaning that God exists within our created world. "The Word became flesh and dwelt among us." Both immanence and transcendence are views of God found in the Bible, making it seem a little schizophrenic at times. In my experience, the God who is "out there" has won out most of the time. God may be with us—but only when we are in church.

If we maintain the "out there" concept of a metaphysical God ruling from the heavens, the world will continue to feel as if it is spinning out of control, with God as an occasional and capricious visitor to our planet rather than an intrinsic part of its ongoing evolution.

one-way tickets to eternity

When theology places God largely outside of our world, the place where God is—heaven—becomes the focus of attention. Over the years, religion's sights have become firmly set on life after death. Who cares about life here—it's only a means to an end. Being ready for heaven is what matters.

But this theological view is more of a modern development of religion than a historical view. The idea of the afterlife was and still is very sketchy in the Jewish faith. Most of the Old Testament is devoid of any real theology about the subject, and it's not until the book of Daniel, one of the later books of the Old Testament, that we find the first concrete mention of the idea. "Multitudes who sleep in the dust of the earth will awake: some to everlasting life, others to shame and everlasting contempt."

In the early years of Christian theology, paradise was the focus. Heaven was the realm of God, but paradise was where humans went after death. The ideological roots of this concept were drawn from a number of other cultural sources. The notion that paradise was found on a mountain overflowing with refreshing springs of pure water was inherited from fourth-century B.C. Israelite ideas and combined with a Persian view of paradise as a walled garden. Eventually, "paradise" was located in the community of the church.

When Jesus said to the thief crucified next to him, "Today you will be with me in paradise," the early Christians thought the resurrection of Jesus confirmed his words—paradise had been reopened here on earth.

But as the theologian Rita Brock has pointed out:

> By the time Columbus plowed the Atlantic, Western Christianity had replaced paradise with purgatory, not only as a destination of the dead, but also as the world Christians inhabited spiritually, on earth, where suffering and austerities led to salvation in the afterlife. Postmortem purgatorial and purifying penalties appeared as a formal doctrine in the Second Council of Lyon in 1274. Masses were said to pray for the deceased, and indulgences were sold to free them from the worst punishments. The dead, instead of being a source of spiritual power to the living, became a spiritual concern and financial burden. The church heaved humanity into a sodden, joyless pit of failure in this life, where no confessions or penances were adequate to wipe away sin, and in the next, where further punishment awaited sinners.

The growing shift toward a theological view of God as somewhere out there, increasingly distant from us, only served to further develop our ideas and thoughts about heaven and hell. Most Christians today have abandoned ideas about purgatory, but we have compensated by elaborating our understanding of hell. Jonathan Edwards, the eighteenth-century preacher, delivered a famous sermon called "Sinners in the Hands of an Angry God" in which he painted a picture of God's anger at "sinners" and the eternal damnation that awaits them.

> O sinner! Consider the fearful danger you are in: it is a great furnace of wrath, a wide and bottomless pit, full of the fire of wrath, that you are held over in the hand of that God, whose

> wrath is provoked and incensed as much against you, as against
> many of the damned in hell. You hang by a slender thread, with
> the flames of divine wrath flashing about it, and ready every
> moment to singe it, and burn it asunder.

I have heard this sermon referenced so many times in the course of
my journey in and with the Christian church, it's no wonder people
can't conceive of a loving God!

But do we really need such an elaborate construct of heaven
and hell in order to have a fruitful and meaningful spiritual life?
Do we have to negate life now, reducing it to a sort of holding tank
until we get somewhere better—or worse? I don't believe so.

saved

One of my favorite movies of the past few years was *Saved!*—a bit-
ing comedy that draws attention to some of crazier aspects of the
evangelical Christian subculture. In the movie, a group of students
at a Christian high school must come to terms with their own fail-
ings and learn to love one another. On many levels, it's a classic
Hollywood feel-good movie, but it also skewers the efforts of many
Christians to make their faith hip and cool ("Are you down with
G-O-D?" asks an overexcited Pastor Skip during the school's opening assembly). It not only challenges Christianity's obsession with
getting people saved—hence the movie's title—but also asks a bigger question: What do we need to be truly saved from? Is it our supposed sinfulness—or bad theology that results in bigotry, judgment,
and self-righteousness?

In one of my favorite scenes, Hilary Faye, the holier-than-
thou leader of an all-girl clique known as the Christian Jewels, kid-
naps Mary, the film's protagonist, and attempts to perform an
exorcism on her when she loses interest in the group. When Mary

resists, Hilary explodes, screaming that she is "filled with Christ's love"—and then she literally hurls a Bible at Mary's head. "The Bible is not a weapon," Mary yells back. But that's just it. For many people, that is precisely what it is.

Because of an overdeveloped sense of both heaven and hell, many people's theology is almost obsessed with our afterlife destination. Christianity is all about getting saved from sin and saved from hell, the punishment for sin. But this is a distortion, or at least a reduction, of the Bible's notion of salvation. The idea of salvation in the Bible encompasses many ideas, including things like bondage and liberation, separation and reconciliation. At its most basic, the word *salvation* means "healing." What it *doesn't* mean is "saved from hell" or "get eternal life when you die." When Jesus said to Zaccheus the tax collector, "Today salvation has come to this house," I am not sure he meant that Zaccheus was guaranteed a spot in heaven. As my friend Brian McLaren has said, the meaning of salvation in the Bible "varies from passage to passage, but in general, in any context, it means to 'get out of trouble.'"

To make salvation simply about what happens when we die is to make it less than it is meant to be. It also makes it conditional, based on one's response to a certain equation or set of beliefs, which is far from the beauty of being connected with God both now and in the future.

The focus on sin is also an issue here. We live in a society that has been washed in a stream of self-help, self-empowerment, and psychology. People process their problems and issues through a wide variety of theories and programs these days like twelve-step groups and support groups. Our common language has lost touch with key theological concepts like sin. It's just not the viable way of connecting people with God that it once was. Sin has become a greatly weakened idea in the hands of the religious because they have made it simply the central cog in the wheel that kicks the salvation machinery into motion. It doesn't really mean much beyond that.

As I see it, a theological emphasis on the afterlife also generates a consumerist attitude toward faith. Everything becomes about evangelizing and gathering souls—a noble idea on one level but troubling on others. (Exhibit A: Mandy Moore wrestling Jena Moore into a van to ensure her eternal destiny in *Saved!*) "Salvation is not a magic formula produced by a secret mixture of sacraments and church membership," notes Vincent J. Donovan, an African missionary whose encounters with tribal Africans challenged him to rethink his own narrow theological views.

A hell-obsessed theology of salvation makes for self-centered humans who actually negate the role and function of grace by striving to corral people into heaven.

Rules and Regulations

Back in college, I was often invited to speak at various Christian youth camps where personal holiness wasn't just encouraged but was mandated. One of the biggest issues was—surprise, surprise—swimwear. At most camps, the rule was modest one-piece bathing suits for girls. "It's what God would have you do," the camps' administrators effectively explained. Then when one-piece styles started to get a little skimpy on the bottom, the rules changed to allow bikinis—but only if they weren't cut too high on the thigh. Did God's mind change?

At other camps, the rule was bikinis with T-shirts over them. But not white T-shirts or even cream-colored T-shirts. They had to be a dark color. Who knew God was so picky about color?

Still other camps prohibited coed swimming altogether. You know what the Bible says about avoiding temptation. It's like that old joke: "Why do Baptists forbid sex while standing up? Because it might lead to dancing."

The rules didn't make any sense then, and they seem just as flawed now. Ephesians says, "For it is by grace you have been saved, through faith—and this is not from yourselves, it is the gift of God—not by works, so that no one can boast." But staying in God's good graces seems to be a different matter.

Performance-driven faith is all about making sure one's life is up to standard, right down to wearing a T-shirt of the right color. It undoes the idea of grace, because it makes grace contingent on other forces.

A performance-based theology sends a terrible message to our insides. It tells us that if we screw up, we might endanger our souls, so life becomes about making sure we are meeting all the requirements. It's the very kind of outward focus Jesus railed against in Matthew's gospel:

> "Woe to you, teachers of the law and Pharisees, you hypocrites! You shut the kingdom of heaven in men's faces. . . .
>
> "Woe to you, teachers of the law and Pharisees, you hypocrites! You travel over land and sea to win a single convert, and when he becomes one, you make him twice as much a son of hell as you are. . . .
>
> "Woe to you, blind guides! You say, 'If anyone swears by the temple, it means nothing; but if anyone swears by the gold of the temple, he is bound by his oath. . . .'
>
> "Woe to you, teachers of the law and Pharisees, you hypocrites! You give a tenth of your spices. . . . But you have neglected the more important matters of the law—justice, mercy and faithfulness. . . .

"Woe to you, teachers of the law and Pharisees, you hypocrites! You clean the outside of the cup and dish, but inside they are full of greed and self-indulgence. . . .

"Woe to you, teachers of the law and Pharisees, you hypocrites! You are like whitewashed tombs, which look beautiful on the outside but on the inside are full of dead men's bones. . . .

"Woe to you, teachers of the law and Pharisees, you hypocrites! You build tombs for the prophets and decorate the graves of the righteous. . . ."

If meeting rules and requirements were really all it took for our theology to mean something, Jesus might have been a little less intense with the religious leaders of his day. After all, they seem to have covered just about every single issue of faith they could create as a condition for right relationship with God. But for Jesus, it wasn't enough. Or perhaps I should say it was too much—of the wrong thing!

When a view of God becomes about paying attention to all kinds of requirements, there is little time left to focus on what all religions teach are the important things—justice, mercy, compassion, goodness, grace, love. It can also feel like you are always on trial. With all those rules, you inevitably feel like you've done something wrong.

When God is viewed as judge and lawgiver, sin becomes the focus. Salvation is salvation from sin. Freedom is freedom from sin.

> paying attention to all kinds of requirements, there is little time left to focus on the important things—justice, mercy, compassion, goodness, grace, love.

Everything related to life and faith gets forced through one particular lens: sin.

Exclusive Theology

Theologies that are heavily oriented toward the afterlife and based on human performance also tend to be exclusive in nature. They begin by making God exclusive, denying that God can be known elsewhere. This leads to a negative regard for people who hold different views and effectively results in limits placed on where, when, and with whom God may communicate.

Consider the early Jewish followers of Jesus. They were surprised that people from outside the Jewish faith could encounter "their" God. But Peter had a dream in which he was commanded by God to eat foods forbidden by Jewish faith. Peter was awakened from this dream by an invitation to visit a Roman centurion who had already encountered Peter's God. In this moment of epiphany for Peter, he explained to the crowds, "You are well aware that it is against our law for a Jew to associate with a Gentile or visit him. But God has shown me that I should not call any man impure or unclean." It was a turning point for the early Christian church.

An exclusivist theology is based on a clear line between the insiders and everyone else. People are easily labeled and categorized, based on where they fit in the particular theological view. The theology advances by converting outsiders into insiders. It's an opt-in version of religion that turns faith into a necessary requirement in order to receive grace. Faith becomes a work, and grace is the carrot held out in front of the person's face.

Faith is many things, but it is not a requirement. It is faithfulness, the giving of oneself, trust in God, and belief that something greater than the material world exists for all of us. Any other interpretation of faith diminishes the gift of grace and places hurdles between God and humanity. In reality, nothing stands between us and God's grace.

In Luke's account, we find the wonderful story of the woman who wiped Jesus' feet with her hair:

> Now one of the Pharisees invited Jesus to have dinner with him, so he went to the Pharisee's house and reclined at the table. When a woman who had lived a sinful life in that town learned that Jesus was eating at the Pharisee's house, she brought an alabaster jar of perfume, and as she stood behind him at his feet weeping, she began to wet his feet with her tears. Then she wiped them with her hair, kissed them and poured perfume on them.
>
> When the Pharisee who had invited him saw this, he said to himself, "If this man were a prophet, he would know who is touching him and what kind of woman she is—that she is a sinner."

The story illustrates how easy it is to make determinations about people based on our understanding of whether they are "in" or "out" of our theological grid. Obviously, a Pharisee would look upon a woman of questionable background with some suspicion. His view of her even affects his opinion about Jesus. He is quite sure that Jesus cannot be the prophet some say he is because a true prophet would know her kind and never allow her to touch him.

The drama in the story is incredible. "Then he turned toward the woman and said to Simon, 'Do you see this woman?'" How could Simon not see the woman? But the point is that he couldn't see past the label he had assigned her. He was practicing a theology of exclusivity and dehumanization disguised as righteousness and purity. Whenever we use dismissive labels to define people—"terrorists," "baby killers," "homos," and the like—they blind us, and we miss the person God loves.

INTERACT ONLINE
Salvation—opt in or opt out? What do you think?

www.spencerburke.com/heretic/salvation

Nostalgia Theology

Give me that old time religion
'Tis the old time religion,
'Tis the old time religion,
And it's good enough for me.

It was good for our mothers.
It was good for our mothers.
It was good for our mothers.
And it's good enough for me.

Makes me love everybody.
Makes me love everybody.
Makes me love everybody.
And it's good enough for me.

It has saved our fathers.
It has saved our fathers.
It has saved our fathers.
And it's good enough for me.

It will do when I am dying.
It will do when I am dying.
It will do when I am dying.
And it's good enough for me.

It will take us all to heaven.
It will take us all to heaven.
It will take us all to heaven.
And it's good enough for me.

Give me that old time religion
'Tis the old time religion,
'Tis the old time religion,
And it's good enough for me.

Many people think the best days of human life were in the past. Not the historical past, necessarily (I don't think too many people want to go back to the Middle Ages!), but certainly the recent past. Some long for the *Ozzie and Harriet* years when widely shared values made our society more genteel or when *Rebel Without a Cause* caused such a stir. Others even have nostalgia for the disco era. In any case, there seems to be a belief that life back then trumps what we experience today.

To be sure, religious tradition offers us a wealth of history to draw strength and inspiration from. Parts of it are indeed wonderful. But there's a difference between respecting the past and waxing lyrical about it. You often hear preachers talking about the New Testament church as a model for how a church is supposed to be. But guess what: there wasn't "a" church in the New Testament—there were lots of different ones. According to the Bible, some were pretty good and some were messed up. But were those days better than today? I don't think so.

Nostalgia is primarily a response to shifting moral ground. It idealizes the recent past—usually the first half of the twentieth century—and dismisses the present day. *Nostalgia* comes from two Greek roots that together mean "pain to return home." In the right circumstance, nostalgia reminds us that there is something beautiful and complete we are meant to experience. But when a theology makes another era of human history better than the one we find ourselves in now, it only confuses things.

When theology gets frozen in history, it becomes a relic of a bygone age that has kitsch value to most people. It's a bit like *That '70s Show* on the Fox TV network. The show parodies the 1970s, but it's not the real 1970s—just a theatrical estimation that attempts to capture a moment but is not applicable in our own lives.

"Old-time religion" is just that—religion for old times, not for new.

Love Not the World

For God so loved the world that he gave his one and only Son, that whoever believes in him shall not perish but have eternal life.

Do not love the world or anything in the world. If anyone loves the world, the love of the Father is not in him. For everything in the world—the cravings of sinful man, the lust of his eyes and the boasting of what he has and does—comes not from the Father but from the world. The world and its desires pass away, but the man who does the will of God lives forever.

It is possible to read both of these passages of Scripture and wind up totally confused. It's no wonder that such a wide range of opinions are held. How can these sayings even be in the same book? The seeming disconnection between the two ideas—a God who loves the world and yet wants us to have nothing to do with it—sets the stage for a problematic view of the state of things. But perhaps the source of the problem is that our reading of these verses is influenced by other concepts. None of us reads Scripture, or any other text, without bias. It seems to me that the apparent tension between these ideas is related to shifts in the way we view God and consequently the world around us.

In the last year of the eighteenth century, a theologian by the name of Friedrich Schleiermacher published a book called *On Religion: Speeches to Its Culture Despisers*. It was his attempt to address a segment of the intelligentsia who looked on religion with disdain because of their love affair with Enlightenment thinking. Schleiermacher tried to emphasize the importance and validity of talking and thinking about faith. More than two centuries later, we have a reversal of sorts. The culture despisers are now, for the most part, those who hold particular theologies and seem to think that in order to love and serve God, they must despise the world and everything in it.

The logic at work here goes all the way back to my first couple of points about God being viewed as outside the world and the companion idea that our destiny lies in heaven, not here on earth. This teaches us that meaning is found elsewhere than this world, so it is no wonder that many people have little regard for the "world."

The oft-used passage from 1 John, a book in the New Testament, that I quoted would seem to validate a low view of the world, but let's think about it for a second. "Everything in the world—the cravings of sinful man"—includes eating and drinking and sleeping and wearing clothes or whatever your body desires to do. "The lust of his eyes" probably includes the desire of anything you want to buy or possess—good, bad, or indifferent—and the "boasting of what he has and does" encompasses anything we boast about or seek after including fighting for station, promotion, or advancement. All of this, the writer says, is "not from the Father but from the world." So what can be done? What exactly does he mean? It seems to me that he means that everything is worldly if your attitude is worldly, but if your attitude is "from the Father," rooted in your theological view of God and life, nothing is worldly. The New Testament says that we should do everything for the "glory of God."

Unfortunately, that's seldom how the passage is read. Instead, it's often used to justify removing ourselves from participating in one of faith's great gifts to humanity—offering patterns of challenge and transformation for the world. Part of faith's role in society is to inject a vision of another way of being human. Jesus did this with his parables. They challenge the way we are living now and offer a path to transforming our lives in the future. A theology that despises the world sacrifices this gift.

> part of faith's role in society is to inject a vision of another way of being human.

Way back in the beginning, according to the book of Genesis, God made the world and then handed it over to humanity to care for and protect. The world was gifted to us, and to equate faith in God with the rejection of the world is to miss part of faith's purpose.

Down with culture

Similarly, a low view of the world and its systems naturally leads to a negative view of world cultures. This is particularly true for many Protestant Christians who hold a low view of the arts and culture in general. This is changing a little as younger people, who have been born in the amniotic fluid of media culture, integrate it into their faith lives, but it is still a point of contention for many people.

The core issue for many people is that they think culture represents a belief system that differs from their own. This potentially narrow view dominates many faiths. I regularly hear people of faith speak about a "secular humanist" culture engaged in a war with the religious community. There is a deep-seated sense of vulnerability and a feeling of being under some kind of attack from culture, but this is a misread. We live in a society actively engaged in the pursuit of meaning, God, and faith.

Culture is more than what we believe. Culture includes knowledge, art, laws, customs, and a host of others things that are the manifestation of what human beings, as members of society, are and what they do.

worms and worm food

"I no longer call you servants, because a servant does not know his master's business. Instead I have called you friends, for everything that I learned from my Father I have made known to you."

Augustine was the first person who made a systematized response when it came to reconciling humanity's call to live in compassion and grace and our apparent inability to do so consistently. Augustine traced the problem all the way back to the book of Genesis and its story of Adam and Eve in the Garden of Eden. Adam's sin in the garden, eating the forbidden fruit, affects us all, he said, because we are all descendants of the original couple. According to him, this "original" sin explains why we are incapable of goodness. In fact, he said, we are tragically unable not to sin—"*non posse non peccare.*" To put it in contemporary language, we are hardwired for sin. Even free will can't help us. Augustine said, "Free choice alone, if the way of truth is hidden, avails for nothing but sin."

Augustine's view of things has captured the imagination of much of Western theology ever since. Of course, Augustine went on to say that God's grace was the only answer, but this part of his equation hasn't received much press. Instead, the view that people are rotten to the core and incapable of any goodness whatsoever has become popular. This is a gross misinterpretation of human brokenness and failing. We are all flawed, that's for sure, but it doesn't mean we are not capable of living lives of meaning and compassion.

Theologies that see no good in people tend to breed strange followers. I say strange because these people often seem unable to truly trust themselves—after all, they have been told they are fatally flawed. In turn, these individuals become dependent on their religion and their religious leaders to do their thinking for them rather than taking responsibility for their lives and living with passion. The "glory of God is a human being fully alive," said Iranaeus hundreds of years ago—alive to the world, alive to ourselves, and alive to God.

All we Need
is Grace

One must have chaos in oneself in order
to give birth to a dancing star.
—Friedrich Nietzsche

An honest religious thinker is like a
tightrope walker. He almost looks as though
he were walking on nothing but air. His
support is the slenderest imaginable. And
yet it really is possible to walk on it.
—Ludwig Wittgenstein

In the twelfth century, Joachim of Fiore was the abbot of Corazzo, Italy. Like many monks of his time, his primary occupation was writing commentaries on the Bible. When it came to the book of Revelation, he couldn't figure out the meaning of its symbolism and spent months "wrestling," as he called it, with the text. One Easter morning, he was given a revelation about the book of Revelation and the relationship between all the books in the Bible. He called this *spiritualis intelligentia*, a spiritual understanding, and used the insight to produce one of the most important commentaries ever written about Revelation.

Joachim's view was simple. Drawing on a Trinitarian concept of God (Father, Son, Holy Spirit), he declared that human history was divided into three distinct eras. The Old Testament was the time of the Father. The New Testament was the time of Jesus. The third phase—still to come—would be a phase of the Holy Spirit.

Using symbols to define each of these periods of history, he created images of the "tree circles," where the two trees representing the Jewish people and the Gentile people grow together through the three ages of history, to make his point. His view was quite utopian, a vision of all humanity drawn together in a form of contemplative monasticism. He wrote that the hierarchy of the church would be unnecessary in this age of the Spirit and that "infidels" (those outside the Christian faith) would unite with Christians.

Joachim figured that this new age would dawn around the year 1200 or so, but it seems not to have happened. However, perhaps Joachim was just a few hundred years off in his calculations. Perhaps we're moving into the "age of the Spirit" today.

For months, my working title for this book was *Heresies I Think I Believe*. The plan was simple: write a series of stand-alone chapters covering all the crazy ideas I had that went against the rules of religion and the teachings of the institutional church. But over time, my vision for the project changed.

Today, I see those ideas—those heresies—as stepping-stones on the path to a new way of being with God in the world. I call this new way "mystical responsibility."

far away, so close

Douglas Coupland playfully points out: "GOD IS NOWHERE / GOD IS NOW HERE / GOD IS NOWHERE / GOD IS NOW HERE." "The whole earth is full of his glory," Isaiah chimes in. "For since the creation of the world God's invisible qualities—his eternal power and divine nature—have been clearly seen, being understood from what has been made, so that men are without excuse," we are told in Romans 1:20.

I no longer believe in an *X-Files* God. What I mean is, I no longer believe "the truth is out there"—or "up there," as the case may be. What's more, I'm not sure I believe in God exclusively as a person anymore either.

Some traditional Christians might grimace when they hear me say that because they cherish a view of God as Father, but even Jesus declared, "The Spirit of the Lord is on me" in Luke's gospel when he launched into his preaching mission in Galilee. The truth is that seeing God as spirit more than person doesn't destroy my faith. In fact, in many ways it makes it stronger.

I now incorporate a panentheist view, which basically means that God is "in all," alongside my creedal view of God as Father, Son, and Spirit. For the record, panentheism is not the same as pantheism, the view that God and the universe are one and the same. Rather, panentheism is like saying God is the ocean and we are the fish in it. God is still God, separate from us but here, close to us, not far away. It relates to the idea of immanence touched on in Chapter Eight—the idea of "God with us," as the introduction of John's gospel says. The apostle Paul even hinted at the idea in Acts: God "is not far from each one of us. 'For in him we live and move and have our being,'" he told a group of seekers in Athens.

As I see it, we are in God, here on earth. This is how our relationship is defined. God does not just have to be reached up to; he is here as the surrounding Spirit.

A panentheist view points to the radical connectedness of all reality and infuses the world with the idea that all life is sacred and therefore to be nurtured and cherished. It is a relational theology that declares that God is to be found *in* the world with us, not just when we get our ticket to heaven. Panentheism fits well with the increasing emphasis on faith as something firmly rooted in this world.

For many people today, the way God is described by traditional faiths can be a struggle. But the concept of God as Spirit, present in our world and wanting to connect with us, and the companion view of life as sacred, is a more accessible way to help people think about faith. A panentheist view of God is broad enough to include ancient faiths, new traditions, and theologies from both East and West—and I like the sound of that. I like the wonderful, creative opportunities that it affords.

i'm a universalist who believes in hell

"I am the true vine, and my Father is the gardener. He cuts off every branch in me that bears no fruit, while every branch that does bear fruit he prunes so that it will be even more fruitful. You are already clean because of the word I have spoken to you. Remain in me, and I will remain in you. No branch can bear fruit by itself; it must remain in the vine. Neither can you bear fruit unless you remain in me.

"I am the vine; you are the branches. If a man remains in me and I in him, he will bear much fruit; apart from me you can do nothing."

One of my other earlier titles for this book was *I'm a Universalist Who Believes in Hell.* The problem is that when I say "universalist," I say it with tongue firmly planted in cheek—and frankly, I couldn't figure out how to do that on a book cover. Do I think "all roads lead to God" or "all religions are basically saying the same thing"? No. I think it's pretty clear that all religions are *not* saying the same thing. There are big differences between many of them, and in fact, sometimes they seem to be going in entirely opposite directions. A belief in reincarnation is not the same as other ideas about what happens after death, for instance.

Nevertheless, I'm attracted to universalism insofar as it acknowledges that many of the world's religions contain true and valuable insights. On the other hand, universalism, as it is traditionally understood, still focuses on religion as the way forward, and I do not. I don't believe any single religion owns heaven or God—even a religion that tries to include everyone.

When I say I'm a universalist, what I really mean is that I don't believe you have to convert to any particular religion to find God. As I see it, God finds us, and it has nothing to do with subscribing to any particular religious view.

The theologian William Barclay once wrote, "The only victory love can enjoy is the day when its offer of love is answered by the return of love. The only possible final triumph is a universe loved by and in love with God." He meant, I think, that all too often our response to God's loving grace has been religion. We've invented and created all kinds of rituals, rites, and traditions to demonstrate that we've "got the message." We're all connected and beloved by God—through religion.

Frankly, I don't see my role as being a gatekeeper for God, presuming to determine who gets in to heaven—and I don't think it's anyone else's role either. To me, theologies that focus on hell are counterproductive to the mission of God because they make life all about what happens to us after death. I don't believe any religion can offer guarantees about things like that. To "guarantee" that someone will go to heaven simply because the person has accepted a set of propositional ideas gives false hope and sets humans up to confer what only God can guarantee.

> All too often our response to god's loving grace has been religion.

Universalism, as it's traditionally understood, is an attempt to offer another way of understanding the world. If you think about it, there is a certain madness to the idea that members of only one religious group can make it into heaven because they happen to know Jesus or some other religious figure. If you are religious and do not hold to some kind of universalist view, then you have two options.

You can either believe that heaven will be filled exclusively with people of your particular faith (a sentiment heard time and again on television), or you can find a way to reconcile your belief in a good and loving God who works things out in ways beyond our understanding.

Universalism says that a theology of grace implies salvation for all, because if grace could be granted only to some people and not to others, based on an arbitrary issue of culture, geography, and luck, it is in fact no grace at all. I concur with that idea, but I also believe that we must take the concept one step further and realize that grace is bigger than *any* religion.

INTERACT ONLINE
If God is loving, how could God let someone choose hell?

www.spencerburke.com/heretic/choosehell

The Highway to Hell

I may be a universalist, . . . but I also believe in hell. Do I mean a place filled with fire, brimstone, and flames that burn bodies forever in eternal torment? No. If I did, that would run counter to everything I have said about God so far. The theologian Clark Pinnock puts it this way: "[The] traditional understanding of hell is unspeakably horrible. How can I imagine for a moment that the God who gave his son to die for sinners because of his great love for them would install a torture chamber somewhere in the new creation in order to subject those who reject him to everlasting pain?"

As the theologian Brian McLaren rightly notes, "More significant than any doctrine of hell itself is the view of God to which one's doctrine of hell contributes." The God I connect with does not assign humans to hell.

And yet I do think it's possible to reject God's grace. There is a strange little verse tucked away in Matthew's gospel that reads this way: "He who is not with me is against me, and he who does not gather with me scatters. And so I tell you, every sin and blasphemy will be forgiven men, but the blasphemy against the Spirit will not be forgiven." Theologians have wrestled with this one for a long time, and it does suggest some kind of action that can exclude someone from God's grace. I certainly don't want to build a case for hell on the basis of one snippet of Scripture, but I do think it brings up an interesting point.

Traditionally, of course, this verse has been one of the church's favorite weapons to force the issue of conversion. "There is no middle ground," well-meaning Christians say. "You are either for Jesus or against him, and he is drawing a line in the sand." And yet, is that really what this verse means? I don't think so. And even if it did mean that, most people I know are not against Jesus. What they resist is the religion that has built up around his name. If resisting religion is the same as resisting Jesus, they may be in trouble, but I don't believe it is.

> Most people i know are not against jesus. what they resist is the religion that has built up around his name.

In another situation, the disciples came to Jesus and told him a man was performing unsanctioned exorcisms and using his name. They had stopped him because the man was "not one of them." "'Do not stop him,' Jesus said. 'No one who does a miracle in my name can in the next moment say anything bad about me, for whoever is not against us is for us. I tell you the truth, anyone who gives you a cup of water in my name because you belong to Christ will certainly not lose his reward.'"

> The famous sin against the spirit can't be simply about rejecting religion—because Jesus himself did that!

Two things stand out to me in this passage. One, anyone who is not against God is for him. Two, it *is* possible to be against God. Somehow or another, it seems that God allows people the freedom to reject grace and "opt out." What does opting out look like—and what does it really mean? Because our task is not to say who is in or out, there is no way of humanly giving a definitive answer to this question. All I know is that the famous sin against the Spirit can't be simply about rejecting religion—because Jesus himself did that!

How these ideas fit together in the grand scheme of things is hard to say. As I said in earlier chapters, God's business is God's business. Heaven and hell are God's domain, and it's not anyone's job to govern them. In fact, in Matthew 13, Jesus makes a point of saying we can actually do more damage than good when we try to get involved in separating "the wheat from the tares" or who is in and who is out.

People often ask how a loving God can send people to hell. My response is that I don't think God does. I do, however, believe that God allows people to choose hell—whatever that might be. Thomas Pendleton, one of the stars of the reality television show *Inked*, said in a recent episode, "Hell to me is being separated from love." Is that what hell is? Is it something more? I don't know. But regardless, I think hell is a choice and not a sentence meted out by God.

As a parent, I find myself allowing my children to make more and more of their own choices these days. As I see it, it's actually love on my part that allows them this freedom. Call it good parenting or common sense, but I think it's good for them to have choices in their lives. Would it cause me amazing pain if my children used their freedom to reject me? Absolutely. But that's the risk I'm willing to take, and I think God gives us the same freedom.

You're in unless you choose to be out

When one of those at the table with him heard this, he said to Jesus, "Blessed is the man who will eat at the feast in the kingdom of God."

Jesus replied: "A certain man was preparing a great banquet and invited many guests. At the time of the banquet he sent his servant to tell those who had been invited, 'Come, for everything is now ready.'

"But they all alike began to make excuses. The first said, 'I have just bought a field, and I must go and see it. Please excuse me.'

"Another said, 'I have just bought five yoke of oxen, and I'm on my way to try them out. Please excuse me.'

"Still another said, 'I just got married, so I can't come.'

"The servant came back and reported this to his master. Then the owner of the house became angry and ordered his servant, 'Go out quickly into the streets and alleys of the town and bring in the poor, the crippled, the blind and the lame.'

"'Sir,' the servant said, 'what you ordered has been done, but there is still room.'

"Then the master told his servant, 'Go out to the roads and country lanes and make them come in, so that my house will be full. I tell you, not one of those men who were invited will get a taste of my banquet.'"

Often context is everything, and in this case, Jesus had been having dinner with a Pharisee. During the course of the meal, he made a point of encouraging those gathered to invite outcasts to their table whenever possible, for they would be repaid by God at the "resurrection of the righteous." In reply to this statement, one of the guests offered the sycophantic remark that those who will be at the "feast in the kingdom of God" are the truly blessed. The inference was that his religious pedigree guaranteed him a place at God's table. At that, Jesus told a story that said just the opposite — a comfortable and expectant religious life might just keep them *out* of the party.

In my experience, this story is often used as a way of getting people to be kind to the less fortunate, but Jesus had already taught that lesson in his original banquet story. This second story seems to be about something else altogether. Jesus turns their whole religious world upside down when he says that none of the people who had the "right" to be at the party went, and conversely, those who did go to the party had no right to be there at all. The truth is that none of us deserve grace, and nothing we do will earn grace. It is ours simply because God has invited us to the party. We're in unless we choose to be out. That is how grace works. We don't opt in to it — we can only opt out.

There is no reason, outside of grace, for grace. We don't get grace because we're sinners or because we have recited the right double-whammy prayer. Grace is a gift.

The wildest part of the story is the very end. After gathering as many people off the streets as they could, there was *still* room at the feast. So the host sent his servants out again to drag people in off the streets. Why? The host would only be satisfied if he had a house full of people.

Grace wants everyone to come to the party. It's a wild bash, not a sedate country club luncheon for members only. It's a rave — a wild, uncontrollable, raucous celebration of God's desire to connect with us.

who really is a prodigal?

Jesus followed up the story of the banquet with another one that further drives the point home.

"There was a man who had two sons. The younger one said to his father, 'Father, give me my share of the estate.' So he divided his property between them.

"Not long after that, the younger son got together all he had, set off for a distant country and there squandered his wealth in wild living. After he had spent everything, there was a severe famine in that whole country, and he began to be in need. So he went and hired himself out to a citizen of that country, who sent him to his fields to feed pigs. He longed to fill his stomach with the pods that the pigs were eating, but no one gave him anything.

"When he came to his senses, he said, 'How many of my father's hired men have food to spare, and here I am starving to death! I will set out and go back to my father and say to him: Father, I have sinned against heaven and against you. I am no longer worthy to be called your son; make me like one of your hired men.' So he got up and went to his father.

"But while he was still a long way off, his father saw him and was filled with compassion for him; he ran to his son, threw his arms around him and kissed him.

"The son said to him, 'Father, I have sinned against heaven and against you. I am no longer worthy to be called your son.'

"But the father said to his servants, 'Quick! Bring the best robe and put it on him. Put a ring on his finger and sandals on his feet. Bring the fattened calf and kill it. Let's have a feast and celebrate. For this son of mine was dead and is alive again; he was lost and is found.' So they began to celebrate.

"Meanwhile, the older son was in the field. When he came near the house, he heard music and dancing. So he called one of the servants and asked him what was going on. 'Your brother has come,' he replied, 'and your father has killed the fattened calf because he has him back safe and sound.'

"The older brother became angry and refused to go in. So his father went out and pleaded with him. But he answered his father, 'Look! All these years I've been slaving for you and never disobeyed your orders. Yet you never gave me even a young goat so I could celebrate with my friends. But when this son of yours who has squandered your property with prostitutes comes home, you kill the fattened calf for him!'

"'My son,' the father said, 'you are always with me, and everything I have is yours. But we had to celebrate and be glad, because this brother of yours was dead and is alive again; he was lost and is found.'"

This classic tale has long been the staple of evangelistic meetings. A wayward son who wastes his inheritance on wine, women, and song, and winds up humiliated and homeless is the stuff of dreams for those who believe we need to "get right with God." The only problem is that there are two sons in the story, and it's the son who never left home that Jesus seems to focus on. It's crazy. How could the life of the son who never seemed to do anything wrong be the point? And yet when it comes to grace, the unexpected angle is always the one to watch.

The son who came home found his father waiting for him, literally scanning the horizon with an aching heart. He had already decided to ask his father to receive him back into the family, not as a son but as a servant, for he knew he deserved nothing more. But the father would have none of it. Before the son could even apologize, his father ran to him and covered him with hugs and kisses. When the son eventually gave his well-planned apology, his father couldn't have been less interested. Instead, he called his servants to bring clothes and jewelry and to prepare a celebration, because his son was lost and now was found.

As this story demonstrates, even repentance is not necessary to get grace. It came after, not before, the father welcomed his son back into his arms. Religion has made much of the need to repent as a condition for grace, but according to this story, repentance isn't required for grace to be given. We respond to grace because of love. As it says in the Good Book, "We love because we were loved first."

false securities

Although the younger brother certainly had his problems, the behavior of the elder brother seems equally problematic—if not more so. First, he was related, and didn't want to be. When he argued with his father about the party, he chose his words carefully, calling the prodigal his father's son—as if he wasn't related to him. That critical distancing of himself from his own flesh and blood highlights the danger of exclusivity. It always creates boundaries between humans. The elder brother's self-righteousness and religious traditions caused him to lose sight of his common humanity. It's an important lesson to remember.

The elder brother was upset because he felt slighted that his father went to such great lengths to celebrate his other son's return and did nothing for him, the one who stayed home. The father seemed a little taken aback by his son's outrage. "Everything I have is yours. But we had to celebrate and be glad, because this brother of yours was dead and is alive again; he was lost and is found."

But the elder brother couldn't enjoy life because he had rules that he thought should determine how everyone should live. Because his younger brother had never done the "right thing," the older brother felt empowered to judge him—something the father wouldn't allow. Life with father was work for him, and because of that, he had no real understanding of his father and no connection with his brother. He was relationally disconnected—both horizontally and vertically. There was no communion in either direction in his life—not with God and not with the rest of humanity.

As I've said, grace is an opt-out issue, not an opt-in one. God wants us at his party, just because we exist. But now that we are connected to God, we need to demonstrate it by following God in spirit. Jesus said, "By this all men will know that you are my disciples, if you love one another." This is mystical responsibility in the face of grace.

εvanɡelism, Discipleship, and salvation?

"A farmer went out to sow his seed. As he was scattering the seed, some fell along the path; it was trampled on, and the birds of the air ate it up. Some fell on rock, and when it came up, the plants withered because they had no moisture. Other seed fell among thorns, which grew up with it and choked the plants. Still other seed fell on good soil. It came up and yielded a crop, a hundred times more than was sown."

When he said this, he called out, "He who has ears to hear, let him hear."

Then Jesus came to them and said, "All authority in heaven and on earth has been given to me. Therefore go and make disciples of all nations, baptizing them in the name of the Father and of the Son and of the Holy Spirit, and teaching them to obey everything I have commanded you. And surely I am with you always, to the very end of the age."

Institutional faiths have traditionally seen evangelizing and converting people as a basic part of their theological grid. If grace is beyond religion, what does that mean for things like evangelism and conversion?

Once again, it is more a question of perspective than anything else. I would not say there is no value in communicating the blessing of being connected to God, but it depends on what we are communicating.

I live close to a big outdoor shopping area where lots of people go to shop, eat, and see movies. Every weekend for as long as anyone can remember, a handful of people have set up a small sound system and engaged in street preaching. Their approach is pretty straightforward. They draw people into conversation about their views on God and then they tell them why they're wrong and why they're headed for hell unless they repent. It doesn't matter who they talk to. The person is always wrong. Many times, these evangelists seem aggressive and hostile. Meanwhile, all this is done in order to "share the good news." Their primary text is the Ten Commandments and judgment. But what about love? It doesn't seem to factor much in their evangelism, except perhaps as a reward to be received once a person has turned his or her life over to God.

I no longer believe that evangelism means the arguing of propositional ideas about God but rather that it is the telling of one's story. There's a big difference between sitting down with someone and talking about one's life experiences and sitting down with someone and offering them a set of concepts about God on which their eternal destiny is said to depend.

In the parable of the sower, the focus has generally been placed on the sowing of the seed. The assumption has been that Jesus was talking about the task of spreading the message of the kingdom, of God's Word, to those who haven't heard it yet. As I see it, the story *is* about spreading the seed of the kingdom, but who is it that's doing the sowing? God is the farmer sowing seed, and the seed of Jesus has already been sown in the world without any of our help. Once again, it is an example of grace at work. We think God needs our help to get the message out. Jesus contended that the message is already sown. We don't have to save people or convert them. God does that. We just need to live out the story and invite people to follow Jesus as we learn to follow him.

Throughout the history of the church, conversion has happened in a number of ways. In the Bible, entire families were converted at the same time. Others had visions that changed them; still others were confronted by their own greed or pride and were transformed when brought face to face with themselves. And yet, although sudden conversion occasionally occurs in the Bible, it is a "minority experience," as the evangelist Richard Peace said.

Today, Christian evangelism seeks to convert masses of people in an instant, which could be why it doesn't last for a lot of people. I no longer believe in conversion as a one-time event. I believe that we experience a great many conversions throughout the course of our lives. Some of them are more significant and life-changing than others, but every day holds potential for transformation and change.

we experience many conversions in our lives.

some are more significant and life-changing than others, but every day holds potential for transformation and change.

Conversion has been presented as a "turning," usually a turning from sin, and while I am not against that idea, it does predicate the experience on certain human actions and responses. I prefer to view conversion with a forward momentum. I think of it as a "connecting" experience that changes the way I look at and live my life.

Nostalgia for Right Now

"Therefore I tell you, do not worry about your life, what you will eat or drink; or about your body, what you will wear. Is not life more important than food, and the body more important than clothes? Look at the birds of the air; they do not sow or reap or store away in barns, and yet your heavenly Father feeds them. Are you not much more valuable than they? Who of you by worrying can add a single hour to his life?

"And why do you worry about clothes? See how the lilies of the field grow. They do not labor or spin. Yet I tell you that not even Solomon in all his splendor was dressed like one of these. If that is how God clothes the grass of the field, which is here today and tomorrow is thrown into the fire, will he not much more clothe you, O you of little faith? So do not worry, saying, 'What shall we eat?' or 'What shall we drink?' or 'What shall we wear?' For the pagans run after all these things, and your heavenly Father knows that you need them. But seek first his kingdom and his righteousness, and all these things will be given to you as well. Therefore do not worry about tomorrow, for tomorrow will worry about itself. Each day has enough trouble of its own."

A spirituality of mystical responsibility is firmly rooted in the present. It is a connection with God in "real time." Mystical responsibility is not merely adopting theories about God; it is about living in sync and in tune with the sacred rhythm of grace. For me, there is no time like the present. I am happy to talk about the past, to celebrate, embrace, and learn from a wide range of traditions — Christian and otherwise. I'm also willing to agree that this life is not all there is, that something happens after we die. But I don't want to focus on these things to the exclusion of the here and now. I find

> mystical responsibility is not merely adopting theories about god; it is about living in sync and in tune with the sacred rhythm of grace.

the most value in focusing on today—how grace is moving me, how life is speaking to me, and how I might live out the grace I have experienced.

I talked in Chapter Eight about nostalgia theologies that desire to return to a time when, it is presumed, things were more favorable for faith and society was more receptive to traditional representations of belief. I think dwelling on the past is every bit as challenging as worrying too much about the future.

I mentioned earlier that our church—a house church, more than anything—often brings food to a nearby park and shares a meal with whoever happens to be there that day. Many of the people we meet rely on public organizations or churches to provide food, and they know how the game is played, so to speak. They've come to understand that there are certain expectations for their behavior and have learned to act accordingly. Consequently, once they find out we're a church, they automatically move into a rote speech they think we want to hear. It usually begins with something like this: "I used to have successful business, a family . . ." or some other rosy story of the past. Then, if that doesn't seem to be resonating, they'll shift gears to the future and cover the same subjects—jobs, reconnecting with their families, getting stable places to stay. They seem to think if they don't talk about these things—or in some way distance themselves from who they are today—we won't be interested in them anymore. Yes, we want to affirm their hopes, dreams, and desires, but at the end of day, we really just want to be with them, no strings attached. No matter who they are, where they've been, or where they're going tomorrow, the act of sitting on a bench in a public park and sharing a bucket of chicken is, in and of itself, enough. Simply being with each other *is* a sacred moment. "Other people come to *serve* us lunch, but you come and *have* lunch with us," one of the ladies said to me once. Another time, the comment was equally profound: "Other people throw rocks at us, but you throw a party."

The challenge is to find the sacred in simple, mundane moments of today—not the past or the future but today. The challenge of the spiritual is to live fully connected here and now. A commitment to mystical responsibility is a commitment to an evolutionary journey toward personal, social, and communal transformation, where we pay attention to life, listen to its messages, and discover its opportunities.

Reclaim the world

As he approached Bethphage and Bethany at the hill called the Mount of Olives, he sent two of his disciples, saying to them, "Go to the village ahead of you, and as you enter it, you will find a colt tied there, which no one has ever ridden. Untie it and bring it here. If anyone asks you, 'Why are you untying it?' tell him, 'The Lord needs it.'"

Those who were sent ahead went and found it just as he had told them. As they were untying the colt, its owners asked them, "Why are you untying the colt?"

They replied, "The Lord needs it."

They brought it to Jesus, threw their cloaks on the colt and put Jesus on it. As he went along, people spread their cloaks on the road.

When he came near the place where the road goes down the Mount of Olives, the whole crowd of disciples began joyfully to praise God in loud voices for all the miracles they had seen:

"Blessed is the king who comes in the name of the Lord!"

"Peace in heaven and glory in the highest!"

Some of the Pharisees in the crowd said to Jesus, "Teacher, rebuke your disciples!"

"I tell you," he replied, "if they keep quiet, the stones will cry out."

Traditional theologies tend to view the world with a certain disdain. It's often assumed that people outside of religion can't possibly catch sight of what God is doing and that without formalized religion, the world might never see Jesus at all. But this story of Jesus coming into Jerusalem on the back of a donkey would seem to challenge a view like that.

Crowds of ordinary people filled the streets of Jerusalem and recognized Jesus for who he was. This drew the attention of the religious leaders, who told Jesus to rebuke his followers. They wanted him to stop them because they thought the people didn't know what they were talking about. Jesus had not been sanctioned by the system, and they were upset that the common people would dare to make profound theological claims about him.

Instead of agreeing to their request, Jesus basically said there was no point in trying to stop the people. If they didn't praise him, the rocks would start to shout! What Jesus was getting at with this story was that the larger world just might be able to grasp Jesus more easily than the religious community. For religious leaders, he represented changes they didn't want, actions they didn't understand, and teachings that threatened their existence. To the people, he was a symbol of hope that God could be found and met in their world and in their streets, not just in the officially sanctioned environments over which religion held power. This man they would invite to their parties and into their homes. This man they would bring their children to for blessing. This man's feet they would wash with their tears. This man they would listen to, because he stood on their ground and lived in their world.

The theological focus of mystical responsibility seeks to recover all of life for God. It is a theology of the marketplace, not just the sanctuary. It is a theology that's available to everyone, regardless of race, color, or creed.

god goes pop

(Jesus walks)
God show me the way because the Devil try to break me
   down
(Jesus walks with me)
The only thing that I pray is that my feet don't fail me now
(Jesus walks)
And I don't think there's nothing I can do to right my
   wrong
(Jesus walks with me)
I wanna talk to God but I'm afraid cause we ain't spoke
   in so long.

When I was growing up, going to the movies was off limits, and most of the rest of popular culture was suspect at best. Not only has our world reclaimed the spiritual, but it has also resituated it firmly in nontraditional environments. One of the prime locations for theological conversation today is the world of pop culture. In a recent article in the *Los Angeles Times* titled "God's Recurring Role in Hollywood," religion reporter Joanna Connors wrote, "If God is everywhere, then evidently everywhere includes the red carpet and the multiplex. It even includes the one place many evangelical Christians believe harbors Satan himself: Hollywood." Movies today are just as likely to explore spiritual themes as they are other social issues. From *Narnia* to *The Passion of the Christ* to films like *Fight Club*, *Crash*, and *Bruce Almighty*, films are bringing the sacred to a cineplex near you.

Pop culture is the new spiritual environment in our world today, and the language of media culture is quickly replacing other forms of expression when it comes to discussing the sacred. It is not just movies. It is books, too—everything from *The Da Vinci Code* to *The Purpose-Driven Life* examines different ends of the Jesus spectrum, and literally hundreds of other titles focus on religion, spirituality, the sacred, and a host of other ideas related to God and faith.

In pop music, an increasing number of artists—from Madonna to the Rolling Stones—are boldly exploring various aspects of religion and spirituality. One of last year's most popular songs was Kanye West's "Jesus Walks." It challenged the idea that Jesus didn't "walk" with people unless they were in church. It aired regularly on MTV accompanied by three different music videos exploring all kinds of spiritual issues related to religion and hip-hop culture.

Awhile back, our house church went to see an exhibition titled "100 Artists See God" at the Laguna Beach art gallery. One Sunday morning, we met in the lobby of the gallery. Instead of the traditional church bulletin, we were offered the gallery map and descriptions of the artwork. We gave our "offering" in the form of admission and began to wander a contemporary cathedral of individual expressions of God. Each of us saw these expressions of love, compassion, judgment, fear, hope, and redemption in traditional sculpture, paintings, contemporary videos, and mixed media. Everyone lingered at a favorite spot for reflection and meditation. After an hour or so, we gathered for lunch on the beach. Kids and adults alike shared what they had heard and experienced from these expressions about God. That particular day, the walls of an art gallery created our sacred space, our sanctuary.

This is the new world of spirituality in the twenty-first century. You're as likely to find people practicing their faith in an art gallery as in church. "The greatest tragedy of theology in the past three hundred years has been the divorce of the theologian from the poet, the dancer, the musician, the painter, the dramatist, the actress, the movie-maker," notes the French Dominican theologian M. D. Chenu. In our time, it seems that tragedy is being turned around as theologians and artists merge.

And in the End—Grace

And if by grace, then it is no longer by works; if it were, grace would no longer be grace.

Grace is a miracle because it is not controlled, structured, shaped, or handed out by human beings or their religions. Grace is not the result of what we could ever plan or calculate. Grace belongs to no one but God, and because of that, it belongs to us all. Grace says that nothing is sacred and everything is sacred. Grace shakes the world, catches us by surprise, and knocks us off our feet. It is the miracle of miracles.

I believe that Jesus was full of grace and truth, and he is greater than the Christian religion that claims him. When the Bible tells us we will be his witnesses to the "ends of the earth" after the Spirit has come upon us, it does not mean that we force Western religion on others. It means that we are invited to bear witness to how Jesus would nurture and affirm the expressions of God's grace in our world today. Grace is the gift we get to share and celebrate with each other. Grace is the key that unlocks the kingdom. Grace is life. Grace is hope. Grace is the future.

> Grace is a miracle because it is not controlled, structured, shaped, or handed out by human beings or their religions.

This is mystical responsibility: questioning, listening, and living in grace.

Mystical Responsibility

Mystical responsibility is a radically different take on what a relationship with God in this world can look like. Whereas traditional religion and institutional churches stress holding certain beliefs, mystical responsibility emphasizes *living* in faith.

Mystical responsibility highlights how broad and varied our experiences of the sacred can be. It captures our experiences of the sacred, those moments when life opens up in ways we never dreamed possible. It also focuses our lives on the future by offering paths to transformation and change.

whereas traditional religion and institutional churches stress holding certain beliefs, mystical responsibility emphasizes **living** in faith.

It is by no means a complete system, nor is it a shrink-wrapped version of new religiosity. Old concepts, new ideas, and incomplete thoughts and notions mix into its unique outline. Mystical responsibility is a way of orienting ourselves to the sacred without some of the baggage we have accumulated over the years. Above all, mystical responsibility is a journey into the new shape of things.

Resting in Grace

I had an opportunity to talk about this mystical responsibility idea with my father before he passed away. I can still remember my mom calling and asking if I'd come visit because Dad didn't think he was

going to make it. He was in his eighties, and neither time nor medicine seemed to be on his side anymore.

When my brother and I arrived, we took turns staying over-
night with him in the hospital. Some nights, he barely got any sleep
at all. It was hard for him to get comfortable, and he had a chronic
cough because of the fluid in his lungs.

"What are you working on right now?" he asked me one
night in the wee hours of the morning, unable to rest.

So I told him. I told him that I thought grace was an opt-out
rather than opt-in venture and that I no longer believed that life was
about swimming around desperately trying to get the life jacket. I
told him about Alden and Gracie and our church and feeding the
homeless people in the park.

It was so strange. Instead of making sure my father was "right
with God," I found myself telling him that maybe saying any prayer
or performing rites and rituals wasn't what it was all about after all.

"You know, I've tried so hard all these years to please God
and do the right thing," he said at last, "but what you just said makes
so much more sense to me."

From there, the conversation turned to how to make the most
of life today. "Love your brother, . . . find a way to be a part of your
sister's life, . . . cherish your mother, . . . take time with your kids,
. . . care for people," my father urged.

When I talked about the people at the park and doing the
things Jesus did, his face lit up. "That's it. You've found what I
believe."

In the morning, I looked deep into my father's eyes, gave him
a kiss, and left, knowing somehow I'd never see him again. And I
didn't. He died two days later.

Often people tell me that I'm endangering people's eternity
with the ideas in this book. They tell me that I'll feel differently
about religion and salvation and all the rest when I'm staring death
in the face someday. But you know what? I all but saw my dad die,

and there was an amazing sense of peace about it all. He lived an amazingly full life, and he wasn't worried about trying to get into heaven at the end. He had this sense, even before I'd talked about it, that God's grace and love were great enough. Bigger, really, than anything religion could comprehend.

INTERLUDE 4

Torture
and Death

The manner of death to which the Spanish Inquisition subjected its victims was called in Spain an *auto de fe,* or "act of faith," and regarded as a religious ceremony of peculiar solemnity. To invest the act with greater sanctity, the deed was always done on the Lord's Day. The innocent victims of this papal barbarity were led forth in procession to the place of execution. Dressed in the most fantastic manner, the caps and tunics of some were painted with things like flames of hell with dragons and demons fanning the flames to keep them especially alive for the heretics. Priests walked alongside the condemned on their journey to death, thundering in their ears that the fires before them were nothing compared to the fires of hell, which they would have to endure forever.

If any brave hearts attempted to say a word for the Lord or in defense of the truth for which they were about to suffer, their mouths were instantly gagged. The condemned were then chained to stakes. Anyone who confessed to being a true Catholic and expressed a desire to die in the Catholic faith had the privilege of being strangled before being burned, but those who refused to claim the privilege were burned alive and reduced to ashes.

The first *auto de fe* took place in Seville, Spain, in 1481, with the execution of six men and women. The last took place on July 26, 1826, when a schoolmaster named Cayetano Ripolli was executed after a trial, for the charge of practicing deism, that lasted nearly two years. His manner of death: garroting. He was strangled with a piece of wire.

Pope Innocent IV authorized the use of torture in 1252. In Spain, it is estimated that torture was used in about a third of all cases to exact confessions. Since some people questioned whether confessions received under torture were valid, the accused were asked, several hours after their initial confession, to verify what they had admitted under torture. If they refused to validate their confession, they were subjected to more torture.

Popular methods of torture included flogging, burning, the rack, and roasting the victim's feet over burning coals. In Spain and Italy, the *garrucha* was popular. Victims' hands were tied behind their backs, and they were then lifted off the ground by a rope tied around the wrists.

In Spain, water torture (*tortura del'agua*) was often employed. The victim was bound to the rack, head lower than the rest of the body. The mouth was forced open, water was poured in, and any victim who didn't confess promptly would soon suffocate.

conclusion:
Heresy as a
way of Life

In 1952, an art gallery in Glasgow, Scotland, opened an exhibit of new works by Salvador Dalí. The painting that drew the most attention was *Christ of Saint John of the Cross*. The inspiration for this painting was a small drawing made by its namesake, the sixteenth-century Spanish mystic known as Saint John of the Cross. Although art critics largely trashed the painting, the work captured the imagination of the public and became one of the twentieth century's most popular and most frequently reproduced religious images.

The most striking feature of the painting is its use of perspective. Dalí shows Christ on the cross hanging over the world, and yet when you look at the painting, it feels as though you are looking down on Jesus.

According to Dalí, the idea for the work came to him in 1950 in what he called a "cosmic dream" and represented the "nucleus of the atom." He wanted to capture Jesus as the essence of the universe. The painting was also a pointed critique of other attempts to capture the image of Christ in art.

Dalí was troubled by the tendency of artists to use the suffering element of death on a cross as a manipulative tool. Matthais Grunewald's *Crucifixion*, painted for a church altar in the 1520s, was "materialistic and savagely anti-mystical," as far as Dalí was concerned. He, in response, determined to paint Christ with more "beauty and joy than has ever been painted before."

Although the trend toward portraying the suffering of Jesus reached an apex in the Middle Ages, we still see shades of it today. Mel Gibson's *The Passion of the Christ* was also influenced by Grunewald's painting, for instance, and seems to have a similar theological premise: portray the crucifixion in such detail that people feel a connection with Christ's suffering.

But Dalí was opposed to this kind of action. "My aesthetic ambition was completely opposite of all the Christs painted by most of the modern painters, who have all interpreted him in the expressionistic and contortionistic sense, thus obtaining emotion through ugliness," said Dalí. In contrast, he set out to make Christ "beautiful as the God that he is."

Indeed, Dalí seems to have succeeded. Unlike other paintings where Christ is emaciated, deathly pale, and sickly looking, the Christ of *Saint John of the Cross* appears youthful, muscular, and contemporary, more like a male model than the classic image we have come to expect from religious Christian art.

But religious images are always historical and contextual. If you look at paintings of Bible images throughout the ages, the clothing and scenery often reflect the time and location of the artist. The nineteenth-century Scottish realist painter William Dyce created a work called the *Man of Sorrows* in 1860. In it, Jesus has the red hair, beard, and ruddy complexion of a Scotsman rather than the darker features of someone born in Palestine, and the Scottish highlands substitute for the desert landscape of Galilee.

The point is that we always infuse our images of God with the social, cultural, and historical situations in which we find ourselves. A U.K. Web site called ReJesus.com has a section devoted to images of Christ throughout history. It is a fascinating journey into the way we have portrayed this singular figure in such diversity.

> we always infuse our images of god with the social, cultural, and historical situations in which we find ourselves.

It is not only how he looks that has changed over the centuries but also what he represents. The image of a suffering Christ crucified on the cross of human violence may have once connected people to the idea of universal human suffering, but today we are more likely to connect with that idea through photos and images of real-life human suffering and tragedy. The early altarpieces and paintings of Christ's suffering were intended to make us feel sorrow and remorse. Today, we can feel sorrow and remorse simply by watching the TV news and being reminded of what horrors we humans are capable of. As Neil MacGregor, director of the National Gallery in Britain, has noted, the newspaper image of a naked little girl, her body burned by napalm, did as much to turn the tide of American support for the Vietnam War as any image of the crucifix would have done in other ages.

Salvador Dalí understood something that I think we, who are interested in religion, often do not. Our religious needs and points of identification change with the times. Dalí replaced the image of Jesus as suffering Savior from another time and place with the God of beauty and grace. He desired a Christ who represented the nuclear age, so rather than focusing on his body, this painting captures mostly Christ's outstretched arms and bowed head, forming, in Dalí's view, a perfect circle and triangle, the representation of the nucleus of the atom.

Dalí's painting was a Jesus of the 1950s, a Jesus for a world come of age through war and the dropping of the atomic bomb—a world of human achievement and destruction on a level unimaginable in earlier times. His painting would probably have made little sense to people who lived in the plague-washed Europe of medieval times. Their Jesus was emaciated and suffering as they were. They connected with him not through his beauty but through his compassionate suffering with them.

The musician Ben Harper saw Martin Luther King Jr. as a "picture of Jesus" in his song of that name. He shifted the focus away from a direct image of Jesus to the "spirit" of Jesus reflected in the life of a person. Rather than gazing at an attempt to capture Jesus' physical likeness, he looked for the essence of Jesus' nature in a person's life, demonstrated through commitment to Jesus' values.

Since the end of the Second World War, our views of Jesus have changed more quickly, reflecting the rapid changes in our lives. We see Jesus' image in new ways, and our image of him is continually transforming. Changes of focus and perspective are good and necessary. The events and issues of our times—whether plagues, threat of nuclear war, terrorism, or the global AIDS issue—inform our images and perceptions of God.

Like Ben Harper, I have a picture of Jesus. Jesus still means something to me, still frames and shapes my own sacred journey, but he probably means and represents different things to me than he does to others. My Jesus is not simply the Jesus of the church, nor is he just the Jesus of religion. He is not only the Jesus of ancient tradition but also of the unknown future as well. Above all, my Jesus is Jesus the heretic.

And in the end . . .

This book has been an attempt to think out loud about some of the things that have changed in me over the past few years. But it's also an invitation to you to join me on this exploration. Before I close, I want to offer a few things that might help you on your journey.

As I have said more than once in this book, I resist shrink-wrapping ideas and creating neat little marketing devices. So receive the things I say not as formulas to live by but as hints, nudges, and clues that might help you on your way.

First, *everyone should be a heretic.* Our times demand it. These are not the times for conventional wisdom. New ideas for new times are needed now. All around us, imaginative people are re-thinking and reimagining the possibilities of what it means to be human. The historian Arnold Toynbee declared that the twentieth century would be remembered as an age in which human society "dared to think of the welfare of the whole human race as a practical objective." He may have been a little optimistic, but there is little doubt that more and more people are trying to make a difference. Whether it is AIDS, global poverty, refugees, children, or a host of other key global issues, the needs are great, and opportunities to better humanity abound.

Even more encouraging, the mavericks who dare to challenge the traditional approaches are having an impact. Bob Geldof and a raft of actors and rock stars are galvanizing young people behind initiatives to combat AIDS and eradicate global poverty. Russell Simmons and his annual hip-hop summits are combating gang violence and fostering spirituality and awareness among urban youth. Oprah Winfrey has her global philanthropic endeavors. Jeffrey Sachs's alternative views are shaping global economics. Bert Ruttan has transformed the space industry and led the first successful private-sector venture into space.

To be a heretic means to question the status quo. In her book on Buddhism, Alexandra David-Neel quotes the Buddha himself as saying that we should not put our faith

> in traditions, even though they have been accepted for long
> generations and in many countries. Do not believe a thing
> because many repeat it. Do not accept a thing on the authority
> of one or another of the Sages of old, nor on the ground that a

statement is found in the books. . . . Believe nothing merely on
the authority of your teachers and priests.

Systems can help us, but they are not infallible, and they are not the
only way to learn about ourselves and the divine. Ask questions,
research, experience, think, and dare to imagine.

Don't just search for information—seek wisdom. Information
about God is helpful for belief systems, but it is wisdom that trans-
forms us. "Be patient toward all that is unsolved in your heart and
try to love the questions them-
selves," said the poet Rainer
Maria Rilke. "Live the questions
now. Perhaps you will gradually,
without noticing it, live along
some distant day into the answer."
A storehouse of spiritual resources
is held by the great faith traditions
of the world, but a return to past
forms of practice is not enough to
meet all the needs of contemporary society when it comes to the
sacred. In the life of mystical
responsibility I have talked about,
the paradoxes of life provide the
impetus for thinking and experi-
menting with the sacred in new
ways.

> In the life of mystical responsibility . . . , the paradoxes of life provide the impetus for thinking and experimenting with the sacred in new ways.

Break your own rules. Whatever it is that you do, try something different. There are lots of interesting things to experience and
enjoy out there. If you have never practiced meditation, go find a
quiet place and give it a shot. Read from people outside of your tradition, or if you've never done it, read the sacred writings of your
own tradition. Take a Sunday off from church, buy someone lunch,
take a walk on the beach, and take a hike. Color outside the lines.

Visit the sacred space of another faith tradition. You may find it isn't for you, but you might glimpse why it works for someone else.

Karl W. Deutsch was one of the world's foremost social scientists. He devoted his life to the study of war, peace, and national cooperation. He commented that the single greatest power we possess is the "power to change," and the most "reckless thing we can do in the future would be to go on exactly as we have in the past." This is true of our societies, and it is true of us. Part of the reason so many people have lost faith in institutional religion is because those groups are unwilling to change, believing that their resistance is proof of their legitimacy, when the opposite is quite often the case. Willingness to change can lead to transformation on both the personal and the communal level.

Get connected. Humanity has evolved along a single line of progression from closed societies to open societies, according to Karl Popper, one of the great minds of the twentieth century. In closed societies, boundaries were very clear and were held together by family, tribal affiliation, national identity, and common experiences. The way we lived was shaped by traditions and taboos, which, in a sense, did all of our thinking for us. The open society is something else. It is the society of personal choice and personal responsibility. Boundaries are much more flexible and fluid, and members form relationships with other societies and groups beyond their immediate proximity. It is a network society where the impetus and challenge of defining ourselves and forming strong relational bonds is placed firmly on individuals.

We are flooded with choices and sometimes overwhelmed by them. And I don't mean consumer choices as much as I mean choices about how we will live. But many of these choices can also be liberating.

The great gift of institutional faiths in closed societies was that they were social systems as well as belief systems; they formed part of the web that made for human interaction and relationships. We may have evolved beyond religion on many levels, but we still need social networks. A life that celebrates the sacred cannot be lived in isolation if we hope to find completeness.

Aristotle said that human beings become fully human through membership in the *polis,* or city-state. In our increasingly interconnected global culture, the opportunity to connect with people has entered a new realm. The possibilities are boundless for meaningful relationships and an expanded "global" soul.

"Love one another," Jesus said. Connect with the world, and find ways to fill it and yourself with grace.

INTERACT ONLINE
Share your hints for living life as a heretic.

www.spencerburke.com/heretic/livinglife

The journey as the destination

"All my past had been but a prelude to the five years that lay ahead of me," Wilfred Thesiger wrote in *Arabian Sands.*

In the past, the heretic's future was defined by the response of others. History is filled with the names of men and women who rejected tradition, and for them the future was none too bright. But today, the heretic leads us into the new future.

According to Rabbi Marc Gafini, the Hasidic teacher Nachman of Bratislav urged his followers to give up the old, familiar things, which, he said, often comfort us but perhaps no longer transform, and to reach instead for the "thing which is beyond us," the thing we can only reach if we are willing to stretch ourselves forward, to leap into the abyss.

This is what the journey toward grace calls us to. May we all live in interesting times.

notes

Introduction

Thomas Huxley's observation is from "The Coming of Age of *The Origin of Species*," in volume 2 of his *Collected Essays*, published in 1880.

Jacques Derrida's essay "Faith and Knowledge: The Two Sources of 'Religion' at the Limits of Mere Reason" appeared in Jacques Derrida and Gianni Vattimo (eds.), *Religion*, trans. David Webb and others (Stanford, Calif.: Stanford University Press, 1998). The quotation is from p. 56. Erik Davis's words are from his book *TechGnosis: Myth, Magic, and Mysticism in the Age of Information* (New York: Harmony Books, 1998), p. 8.

Anne Rice's novel *Christ the Lord: Out of Egypt* (New York: Knopf) was published in 2005. She was interviewed on NBC's *Today* show on Nov. 1, 2005.

Archibald MacLeish's words are from "Hypocrite Auteur," in *Collected Poems, 1917–1982* (Boston: Houghton Mifflin, 1985), p. 415.

Peter L. Berger's quote is from *The Heretical Imperative: Contemporary Possibilities of Religious Affirmation* (New York: Anchor/Doubleday, 1979), p. 28.

Art Kleiner made his observation in *The Age of Heretics: Heroes, Outlaws, and the Forerunners of Corporate Change* (New York: Currency/Doubleday, 1996), p. x.

Chapter One: Jesus Beyond Christianity
The quote by Bono (Paul David Hewson) is from Susan Black, *Bono: In His Own Words* (London: Omnibus Press, 1997), p. 29.

You can read Dietrich Bonhoeffer's letter "Religionless Christianity" in "Letters to Eberhard Bethge" in *A Testament to Freedom: The Essential Writings of Dietrich Bonhoeffer*, ed. Geffrey B. Kelly and F. Burton Nelson, rev. ed. (San Francisco: HarperSanFrancisco, 1995).

William J. Ventimiglia expressed his views on fundamentalism on p. 66 of "Where Is God Gone?" in *Parabola*, Winter 2005.

Origen's words are from sec. B.8 of Frederick Crombie's translation of "Contra Celsum" [Against Celsius], published in Edinburgh in 1872. This work was reprinted in *The Anti-Nicene Fathers*, volume 4 (Grand Rapids, Mich.: Eerdmans, 1979).

Vincent of Lérins's comment is documented in "The Commonitory of Vincent of Lérins," trans. C. A. Heurtley, ch. 14, para. 44, in Philip Schaaf, *Sulpitius Severus, Vincent of Lérins, John Cassian* (Grand Rapids, Mich.: Christian Classics Etherial Library, 2004).

The quotation attributed to Muhammad is from the entry "Muhammad" in *The Oxford Dictionary of World Religions*, ed. John Westerdale Bowker (New York: Oxford University Press, 1997).

Hans Kung's statement is from *Global Responsibility: In Search of a New World Ethic* (New York: Crossroad, 1991), p. xv.

The journal entry on religion posted Aug. 12, 2005, by Moby (Richard Melville Hall) can be read at http://www.moby. com/moby_archive/1/1/2005/8/7007.

You can read the ideas of Ziauddin Sardar in *Islam, Postmodernism, and Other Futures: A Ziauddin Sardar Reader,* ed. Sohail Inayatullah and Gail Boxwell (Sterling, Va.: Pluto Press, 2003). Those of Parvez Ahmed are recounted in David Schimke, "Taking Back Islam: Parvez Ahmed Says It's Time to Declare a Jihad on Extremism," *Utne,* Nov.-Dec. 2005.

James W. Fowler's *Stages of Faith: The Psychology of Human Development and the Quest for Meaning* (San Francisco: HarperSanFrancisco) was published in 1981.

Giovanni Maria Tolosani criticized Copernicus in "Heaven and the Elements," written in 1546 as an appendix to *On the Truth of Holy Scripture.*

The quote from Sallie McFague is the first line of the Introduction to her book *Speaking in Parables: A Study in Metaphor and Theology* (Minneapolis, Minn.: Augsburg Fortress, 1975).

The expression "the beliefs and ideas that stunt holiness today" is from the Preface to the paperback edition of Douglas Rushkoff, *Nothing Sacred: The Truth About Judaism* (New York: Three Rivers Press, 2004), p. x.

Chapter Two: Grace Beyond Religion
The epigraph by Miroslav Volf is from *Exclusion and Embrace: A Theological Exploration of Identity, Otherness, and Reconciliation* (Nashville, Tenn.: Abingdon Press, 1996), p. 85.

Hinges of History is the title Thomas Cahill has given to his suite of historical books; four of the projected seven volumes have been published so far.

Phyllis A. Tickle's observations on consensual illusions were quoted by Eric Reed in "New Journeys on Well-Worn Paths," *Leadership Journal,* Summer 2005 [http://www.christianitytoday. com/le/2005/003/21.44.html].

Carter Phipps's comment is from his article "Enlightenment Unplugged," *W/E Magazine,* Feb.-Apr. 2006, p. 90.

Cathy Grossman reported on the poll of Americans who view religion in a negative light in her article "Charting the Unchurched in America," *USA Today,* Mar. 7, 2002 [http://www.usatoday.com/ life/2002/2002-03-07-no-religion.htm].

The German philosopher Karl Jaspers introduced the term "Axial Age" in 1949; his book was published in translation in the United States as *The Origin and Goal of History* (New Haven, Conn.: Yale University Press, 1954).

Phyllis A. Tickle's comments on AA have been expressed in many of her speeches and are highlighted in Heidi Schlumpf, "Recovering Grace: Spiritual Wisdom from the 12 Steps," *U.S. Catholic,* Nov. 2003, pp. 12–17.

Elizabeth Debold discusses the division of morality from spirituality in "The Dilemma of Ethics in an Out-of-Control World," *W/E Magazine.* Feb.-Apr. 2004, p. 53.

Karen Armstrong's observations are from *The Battle for God* (New York: Knopf, 2000), pp. xii, xiii.

Robert Farrar Capon's quip is from *The Parables of Judgment* (Grand Rapids, Mich: Eerdmans, 1989), p. 55.

John Drane's book *Do Christians Know How to Be Spiritual? The Rise of New Spirituality and the Mission of the Church* (London: Darton, Longman & Todd) was published in 2005. James Beckford set out his theory in *Religion and Advanced Industrial Society: Controversies in Sociology* (London: Routledge, 1989).

William Blake's verses are lines 172–175 of the poem "The Everlasting Gospel," which he wrote around 1818 or possibly earlier.

Zygmunt Bauman expressed his views on consumerism in *Post-modernity and Its Discontents* (New York: NYU Press, 1997). Barbara Kruger created her "I Shop; Therefore, I Am" poster in 1990, although the phrase may have been around for awhile by then. Robert Bocock's comments are from *Consumption* (New York: Routledge, 1993), p. x.

James B. Twitchell's observation is from *Lead Us into Temptation: The Triumph of American Materialism* (New York: Columbia University Press, 1999), p. 14.

You can view the debate on rebranding God at the Brandchannel Web site [http://www.brandchannel.com/forum.asp?bd_id =8].

The Barna Group's statistics can be found online at the Barna Group Research Web site [http://www.barna.org].

Read about Testamints at the Ship of Fools Web site [http://ship-of-fools.com/Gadgets/Witnessing/015.html].

The largest purveyor of Christian underwear is MissPoppy.com [http://www.jesus21.com/poppydixon/product/panties/panties .html].

Gianni Vattimo's words are from *After Christianity*, trans. Luca D'Isanto (New York: Columbia University Press, 2002), p. 99.

Chapter Three: Grace and the God Factor

The opening quotation is from Diarmuid Ó Murchú, *Quantum Theology* (New York: Crossroad, 1999), p. 21.

"God's Hotel," by Nick Cave: Words and music by Nick Cave. Copyright © 1994 Mute Song Ltd. All rights in the United States and Canada Administered by Windswept Pacific. International copyright secured. All rights reserved. Complete lyrics can be found in Nick Cave's book *King Ink* (London: Black Spring Press, 1993), p. 154.

Ron Sexsmith's lyrics are from "God Loves Everyone," written by Ronald Eldon Sexsmith, © 2002. Published by Ronboy Rhymes, Inc., Sony/ATV Music Publishing.

Jung's thoughts about spirituality are recorded in *Analytical Psychology: Notes of the Seminar Given in 1925 by C. G. Jung,* ed. William McGuire (Princeton, N.J.: Princeton University Press, 1991), p. 106.

The story told by Thich Nhat Hanh appeared in "Beyond Views: An Exchange with Thich Nhat Hanh," an article by Diane Wolkstein in *Parabola,* Winter 2005, p. 21.

Meister Eckhart's quote can be found online at [http://www.near-death.com/experiences/paranormal11.html].

Steven Colbert made his comment on *The Daily Show* on Oct. 12, 2005. The Dalai Lama spoke on *Larry King Live* on Sept. 11, 2005.

The quote from Paul Heelas and Linda Woodward, *The Spiritual Revolution: Why Religion Is Giving Way to Spirituality* (Malden, Mass.: Blackwell, 2005), is from p. 7.

Marshall McLuhan discusses what it means that "God is dead" in his book with Quentin Fiore, *The Medium Is the Massage:*

An Inventory of Effects (Corte Madera, Calif.: Gingko Press, 2001), p. 146. This book was originally published in 1967.

Excerpt from Paul Tillich sermon: From *The Shaking of the Foundations: Sermons by Paul Tillich.* Copyright © 1948 by Charles Scribner's Sons. Reprinted with permission.

E. B. White, in his 1941 essay "Some Remarks on Humor," wrote, "Humor can be dissected, as a frog can, but the thing dies in the process and the innards are discouraging to any but the pure scientific mind." Philip Yancey merely changed the word *humor* to *grace* in *What's So Amazing About Grace?* (Grand Rapids, Mich.: Zondervan, 1997), p. 16.

Douglas John Hall discusses sin in *The Cross in Our Context: Jesus and the Suffering World* (Minneapolis, Minn.: Augsburg Fortress, 2003), p. 104.

Alan Mann's comments are from *Atonement for a "Sinless" Society: Engaging with an Emerging Culture* (Milton Keyes, England: Paternoster Press, 2005), p. 17.

Polly Toynbee reviewed *The Chronicles of Narnia* in "Narnia Represents Everything That Is Most Hateful About Religion" in the *London Guardian,* Dec. 5, 2005.

Michael Dowd's remarks regarding salvation are from his Web site at [http://www.evolutionarychristianity.org/salvation.html].

Joachim Jeremias's comment on the parable of the mustard seed is from *The Parables of Jesus,* 3rd rev. ed. (London: SCMP, 1972), p. 12.

Chapter Four: The End of the World as We Know It
The chapter opening quotation is from "Pete Rollins Pops In for a Drop of the Black Stuff," an interview posted at Stories from the Virtual Café, Oct. 2003 [http://www.emerging church.info/stories/cafe/peterollins/index.htm].

Professor Eddie Gibbs reported the statistics on church attendance
in Britain and the age of U.S. churchgoers in a lecture at
Fuller Theological Seminary on Nov. 26, 2005.

Callum F. Brown's remarks are from *The Death of Christian
Britain: Understanding Secularization, 1800–2000*
(New York: Routledge, 2001), p. 198.

Erik Davis's comments are from *TechGnosis: Myth, Magic, and
Mysticism in the Age of Information* (New York: Three
Rivers Press, 1993), p. 74.

Karl Jaspers's contention that humans have "started from scratch"
four times is from *The Origin and Goal of History*, English
edition (London: Routledge, 1953), pp. 37–38.

Phyllis Tickle's observations on Luther, Spong, and social
developments are from her Emergent Conference
Seminar, held in May 2005 in Nashville, Tennessee.

Douglas Rushkoff's observations are from *Playing the Future:
What We Can Learn from Digital Kids* (New York:
Riverhead Books, 1999), p. 5.

Robert N. Bellah's comments appeared in "Religious Evolution,"
American Sociological Review, 1964, 29, 358–374
[http://trevor.butler.edu/~jwolfe/religevol.txt]. Further
thoughts on this topic can be found in Charles Y. Glock
and Robert N. Bellah (eds.), *The New Religious Consciousness* (Berkeley: University of California Press, 1976).

J. Gordon Melton's quote is from "Modern Alternatives in the
West," in John R. Minneus (ed.), *A Handbook of Living
Religions* (London: Penguin, 1984), p. 455.

Christopher H. Partridge's observations can be found in *The
Reenchantment of the West: Alternative Spiritualities,*

Sacralization, Popular Culture, and Occulture (New York: T&T Clark International, 2006), p. 4.

Barbara Walters's special *Heaven: Where Is It? How Do We Get There?* aired on NBC on Dec. 20, 2005.

Jaspers's remarks on individualization are from *The Origin and Goal of History*, pp. 278–279.

Robert Bellah's thoughts on the future of religion can be found in his book *Beyond Belief: Essays on Religion in a Post-Traditional World* (New York: HarperCollins, 1976).

Joseph M. Kitagawa's observations are from *The History of Religions* (Chicago: University of Chicago Press, 1973), which he wrote in collaboration with Mircea Eliade and Charles H. Long.

Anita Roddick's Web site is, logically enough, http://www.anitaroddick.com.

Mathew Fox's views on the religion in the developed world are expressed in *Creation Spirituality: Liberating Gifts for the Peoples of the Earth* (San Francisco: HarperSanFrancisco, 1991). The quotation is from p. 74.

John Drane discusses church and culture in his book *Cultural Faith and Biblical Faith* (Milton Keyes, England: Paternoster Press, 2000).

Phyllis A. Tickle's comment is from *God-Talk in America* (New York: Crossroad, 1997), p. 9.

Walter Brueggemann's comment on "culture despisers" is from *In Man We Trust: The Neglected Side of Biblical Faith* (Louisville, Ky.: Westminster/John Knox, 1973), p. 14.

The excerpt from Thomas Merton's Calcutta speech is from *The Asian Journal of Thomas Merton* (New York: New Directions, 1973), p. 313.

Richard Holloway's remarks are from "The Freedom to Question," a lecture he delivered at the University of Edinburgh, Scotland, on Feb. 10, 2003.

Chapter Five: Grace Held Hostage

The opening epigraph is from Tom F. Driver, *Christ in a Changing World: Toward an Ethical Christology* (New York: Crossroad, 1981), p. 56.

You can read Tyler Thoreson's article "Marketing God," from the Jan.-Feb. 2000 issue of *Gadfly*, online at http://www.gadfly online.com/archive/JanFeb00/archive-marketing. html.

Peter Harrison's comments are from *"Religion" and the Religions in the English Enlightenment,* new rev. ed. (New York: Cambridge University Press, 2002), p. 11. The later quote from the same work is from p. 174.

Wilfred Cantwell Smith's observation in *The Meaning and End of Religion* (Minneapolis, Minn.: Augsburg Fortress, 1991), is from p. 32.

Graham Ward's comment is from *True Religion* (Malden, Mass.: Blackwell, 2003), p. 7.

Douglas Rushkoff's remarks from *Nothing Sacred* appear on pp. 48–50.

Pat Robertson identified Ariel Sharon's health problems as divine retribution on Jan. 6, 2006.

Noah Levine made these comments on Nov. 16, 2005, during weekly meditation at Dancing Shiva Studio in Los Angeles. His book *Dharma Punx: A Memoir* (San Francisco: HarperSanFrancisco) was published in 2003.

Carter Heyward's words about Jesus are from *Saving Jesus from Those Who Are Right: Rethinking What It Means to Be*

Christian (Minneapolis, Minn.: Augsburg Fortress, 1999), p. 113. The comment later in the chapter on how people read the Bible is from p. 3.

Salman Rushdie was quoted by Chris Heath in "The Second Life of Salman Rushdie," *GQ*, Sept. 2005, p. 405.

Maggi Dawn's remarks are from "I Am the Truth: Text, Hermeneutics, and the Person of Christ," reprinted in *Anglicanism: The Answer to Modernity*, eds. Duncan Dormor, Jack McDonald, and Jeremy Caddick (New York: Continuum, 2003).

Douglas Rushkoff discusses metaphors in his book *Playing the Future* (New York: Riverhead Books, 1999), p. 253.

Beverly W. Harrison objected to "capitalist spirituality" in *Making the Connections: Essays in Feminist Social Ethics*, ed. Carol S. Robb (Boston: Beacon Press, 1985).

The comment on Christendom's carrying the "charge of perpetuity" is from Peter Robert Lamont Brown, *The Rise of Western Christendom: Triumph and Diversity*, A.D. 200–1000, 2nd ed. (Malden, Mass.: Blackwell, 2003), p. 487.

Alan Kreider's insightful work is *The Origins of Christendom in the West* (New York: Clark, 2001).

Kjell Nordstrom and Jonas Ridderstale's thoughts on how hierarchy became sacred are discussed in their book *Funky Business: Talent Makes Capital Dance* (London: Bookhouse, 2000).

Tibor Kalman's comment on religion is from Peter Hall (ed.), *Tibor Kalman: Perverse Optimist* (New York: Princeton Architectural Press, 1998), p. 10.

Sinead O'Connor was quoted in *Q Magazine*, Oct. 2005, p. 117.

Chapter Six: Faith Remixed: The Fine Art of Bricolage

The opening quotation is from Callum G. Brown, *The Death of Christian Britain: Understanding Secularization, 1800–2000* (New York: Routledge, 2001), p. 1.

Salman Rushdie's novel *Shalimar the Clown* (New York: Random House) was published in 2005. The quote is from p. 37.

Jack Miles writes about the Samaritan woman in *Christ: A Crisis in the Life of God* (New York: Knopf, 2001), pp. 63–71.

Max Weber's views on the organization of social systems can be found in *The Protestant Ethic and the "Spirit" of Capitalism and Other Writings*, trans. Peter Behr and Gordon C. Wells (London: Penguin, 2002).

Alan W. Jones's words are from *Reimagining Christianity: Reconnect Your Spirit Without Disconnecting Your Mind* (Hoboken, N.J: Wiley, 2005), p. 20.

Tim Boucher blogged about religion in "Pop Occulture" at his Web site [http://www.timboucher.com].

The quote by DJ Spooky is from Paul D. Miller, *Rhythm Science* (Cambridge, Mass.: MIT Press, 2004), p. 71.

Claude Lévi-Strauss wrote about spiritual bricolage in *The Savage Mind* (Chicago: University of Chicago Press, 1966).

Charlie Rose's interview with Reed Hastings aired on *Charlie Rose*, PBS, Dec. 27, 2005.

Excerpt from *On Beyond Zebra: From On Beyond Zebra* by Dr. Seuss. TM & © 1955, renewed 1983 by Dr. Seuss Enterprises, L.P. Reprinted by permission of Random House Children's Book Publishing.

Chapter Seven: Jesus the Heretic

John F. Kennedy's words are from a speech he gave at Yale
University on June 11, 1962.

The Douglas Rushkoff quote is from *Nothing Sacred: The Truth
About Judaism* (New York: Three Rivers Press, 2003),
p. 200.

Archbishop Rowan Williams's *Writing in the Dust: After September 11* (Grand Rapids, Mich.: Eerdmans) was published
in 2002. The comment about "using other people to think
with" is from p. 64; his thoughts on Jesus and the adulteress
are expressed on p. 78.

Ray Sherman Anderson's conversation between Jesus and Judas
can be found in *The Gospel According to Judas: Is There a
Limit to God's Forgiveness?* rev. ed. (Colorado Springs,
Colo.: NavPress, 1994).

Chapter Eight: The Mystery of God, Grace, and Salvation

Nick Cave's lyrics are from "Into My Arms," written by Nick Cave
and performed by Nick Cave and the Bad Seeds, © 1997
by Mute Song Ltd.

Rita Nakashima Brock's comment is from the lecture "Saving
Paradise," delivered at the 2005 Festival of Homiletics,
Fourth Presbyterian Church, Chicago, May 17, 2005.
Brian McLaren discusses the meaning of salvation in his
book *Generous Orthodoxy: Why I Am a Missional, Evangeli-
cal, Post-Protestant, Liberal-Conservative, Mystical-Poetic,
Biblical, Charismatic-Contemplative, Fundamentalist-
Calvinist, Anabaptist-Anglican, Methodist, Catholic, Green,
Incarnational, Depressed-yet-Hopeful, Emergent, Unfinished
Christian* (Grand Rapids, Mich.: Zondervan, 2004).

Vincent J. Donovan's quote is from his book *Christianity Rediscov-
ered* (Maryknoll, New York: Orbis, 1998).

The lyrics to "Old Time Religion" were first published by the
singing evangelist Charles Davis Tillman before the turn
of the twentieth century; he had heard the song sung by
African Americans attending a camp meeting in South
Carolina.

Chapter Nine: All We Need Is Grace

Friedrich Nietzsche's line is from *Thus Spoke Zarathustra*, trans.
Walter Kaufmann (New York: Modern Library, 1995),
p. 17. The work was originally published between 1883 and
1892. Ludwig Wittgenstein's words are from *Culture and
Value*, ed. G. H. von Wright, trans. P. Winch (Oxford:
Blackwell, 1980), p. 73. They were originally written in
1948.

Douglas Coupland's play on words is from his novel *Hey
Nostradamus!* (New York: Bloomsbury, 2004), p. 7.

William Barclay's quote is from *William Barclay: A Spiritual
Autobiography* (Grand Rapids, Mich.: Eerdmans, 1977),
p. 67.

Clark Pinnock debates the traditional understanding of hell in
"Fire, Then Nothing," *Christianity Today*, Mar. 1987,
p. 40.

Brian McLaren writes about the doctrine of hell in *The Last Word
and the Word After That: A Tale of Faith, Doubt, and a New
Kind of Christianity* (San Francisco: Jossey-Bass, 2005).

Thomas Pendleton gave his definition of hell on the "Trouble in
Paradise" episode of the TV reality show *Inked*, which aired
on A&E on Oct. 12, 2005.

Richard V. Peace calls conversion a "minority experience" in his
book *Conversion in the New Testament: Paul and the Twelve*
(Grand Rapids, Mich.: Eerdmans, 1999), p. 5.

"Jesus Walks," by Kanye West: "Words and Music by Kanye West, Curtis Lundy, Che Smith and Miri Ben Ari. Copyright © 2004 EMI Blackwood Music Inc., Please Gimme My Publishing, Inc., Curwan Music, Song of Universal, Inc., Mirimode Music, BMG Songs and Solomon Ink. All rights for Please Gimme My Publishing, Inc. controlled and administered by EMI Blackwood Music, Inc. All rights for Solomon Ink controlled and administered by BMG Songs. All rights for Mirimode Music controlled and administered by Songs of Universal, Inc. All rights reserved. International copyright secured. Used by permission.

Joanna Connors's article "God's Recurring Role in Hollywood" appeared in the *Los Angeles Times* on Dec. 23, 2005.

M. D. Chenu is quoted in Matthew Fox, *Confessions: The Making of a Postedenominational Priest* (San Francisco: HarperSanFrancisco, 1996), p. 63.

Conclusion: Heresy as a Way of Life
The material on Salvador Dalí is based on "Salvador Dalí's 'Christ of St. John of the Cross' Wins Herald Poll" [http://www.glasgowmuseums.com] and information at the Salvador Dalí Museum's Web site [http://www.salvadordalimuseum.org].

Neil MacGregor's observation is from his book *Seeing Salvation: Images of Christ in Art* (New Haven, Conn.: Yale University Press, 2000).

Ben Harper wrote and performed "Picture of Jesus" on the 1994 CD *Diamonds on the Inside,* © 2002 by EMI Virgin Music/Innocent Criminal Inc. Reprinted with permission.

Anrnold Toynbee's observations about the twentieth century were quoted by Lester Bowles Pearson in "A Study of History,"

Nobel Lecture, Dec. 11, 1957 [http://www.nobelprize.org/peace/laureates/1957/pearson-lecture.html].

Alexandra David-Neel quotes the Buddha in her book *Buddhism: Its Doctrine and Its Methods* (London: Bodley Head, 1977), p. 147.

Rainer Maria Rilke penned his thoughts on seeking wisdom in *Letters to a Young Poet* (1903).

Karl W. Deutsch is quoted in Jennifer Mae Barizo's article "Welcome to the Next Generation," *Adventist Review Online Edition,* Special Millennium Edition [http://www.adventistreview.org/1999-1452/millenn4.html].

Karl Raimund Popper expressed his views on open and closed societies in *The Open Society and Its Enemies,* 4th rev. ed. (Princeton, N.J.: Princeton University Press, 1963).

Wilfred Thesiger's comment is from p. 38 of the 1985 Penguin edition of *Arabian Sands,* which was originally published in 1959.

Rabbi Marc Gafini quoted Nachman of Bratislav in "The Evolution of Divinity: A New Spiritual Vision for Our Time," *W/E Magazine,* Oct.-Dec. 2004, p. 40.

INTERACT ONLINE

Add your recommendations of works that others might learn from.

www.spencerburke.com/heretic/recommendations

the Authors

S pencer Burke is a man of metaphors. *Kindling* describes his approach to speaking and consulting. He sparks new thought and conversation in his audiences and clients through his innovative thinking, humor, compassion, and use of arts and technology. Whether talking to ten or ten thousand, he encourages people to view their businesses and relationships in new ways, and they walk away ablaze with the possibilities.

Cave painting is an ancient tool used to express the stories of the soul. Burke has always been fascinated with individual and collective spiritual stories and has chronicled these through his photography. His work has been collected and exhibited at galleries, and he has taught photography at the university level. He cofounded the Damah Film Festival, exploring spiritual themes. In the 1990s, he created TheOOZE.com, a safe online community for a diverse faith-based population to connect through articles, message boards, and social networking. This community has grown to include over 150,000 monthly visitors from ninety countries. Burke is the author

of *Making Sense of Church* (Zondervan, 2003), in which he con-
trasted his twenty-two years as a pastor in a traditional church with
eight years of exploring emerging, nontraditional metaphors.

Burke has been described as a *heretic.* After achieving more
than he dreamed as a teaching pastor at a megachurch, he refo-
cused on his original desires to love, serve, and live a grace-filled
life. Burke lives out his faith with what the *Los Angeles Times* called
a "church with no name." He developed ETREK, collaborative
learning groups that challenge the individual and traditional educational values. He also initiated Friends of God's Golden Acre in the
United States, to raise awareness and funds for a South African
organization committed to loving, educating, and supporting individuals and families affected by the AIDS epidemic. Spencer
Burke.com is the latest adventure that has him looking for new ways
to evolve.

Burke lives in Southern California with Lisa, his wife of twenty
years, and children Alden, nine, and Grace, five.

Barry Taylor has a master's degree in cross-cultural studies and
a doctorate in intercultural studies, a field in which he has
concentrated on the relationship between popular culture and contemporary spirituality.

Taylor developed and teaches a series of spiritually innovative classes on music, film, and contemporary theology at Fuller
Theological Seminary. In addition, he teaches at the Art Center
College of Design in Pasadena, lecturing in the School of Advertising on design and creativity.

Taylor also writes and performs original music and has served
as a music supervisor and composer for a number of motion pictures. He also leads an ongoing conversation at New Ground in Los
Angeles, a weekly gathering committed to guarding the great questions and engaging contemporary culture with the gospel in alternative ways.

He wrote A *Matrix of Meaning: Finding God in Popular Culture* (Baker Academic, 2003) with Craig Detweiler and is currently working on several new books.

INTERACT ONLINE

Log on to see where the authors will be speaking next or to find out more about bringing them to your event.

www.spencerburke.com/heretic/speaking

scripture index

This index lists all of the Scripture references for all the stories I have quoted from the Bible so that you can look them up and read them for yourselves. I believe it's helpful to look at the stories in the context that they have been given to us. It's easy to take only the verses you agree with from the Bible and build a case for your own particular ideological view. We all have our opinions and feelings about what is important and none of us come to our holy books without some bias. What I have written about in this book is based very much on how I have read, interacted with, and reflected on certain passages and stories, but I have tried to look at them honestly and let them speak to me as much as have them confirm what I want them to say. I hope you'll do the same, and let the stories offer you new perspectives on life, love, and God.

Unless otherwise noted, all Scripture quotations are from The Holy Bible, New International Version.

index